Year 2

Disciples

worship

Ron Rienstra

FAITH
ALIVE®
Christian Resources

Grand Rapids, Michigan

This study is part of *Disciples*, year 2, a comprehensive multiyear faith formation program for adults. Year 2 studies build on the foundation laid by the studies in year 1.

Year 2 includes the following five-session study guides, which feature five daily readings for each session.

- Prayer
- Reading the Bible
- Worship
- Living in Community
- Overcoming Sin

Unless otherwise indicated, Scripture quotations in this publication are from the Holy Bible, Today's New International Version, © 2001, 2005 by the International Bible Society. All rights reserved worldwide. Used by permission.

We welcome your comments. Call us at 1-800-333-8300 or e-mail us at editors@faithaliveresources.org.

Contents

Introduction

Kitchen Lessons

"Taste and see that the LORD is good."

—Psalm 34:8

My daughter loves cookies. She loves to eat them (of course!) and now that she's old enough, she enjoys learning how to bake the family favorites herself. One of the things she's learned right away is that a recipe leaves a lot of important stuff out. My wife or I have to show her; we have to work through the steps together.

As long as we follow the recipe exactly, it's all good. But as young people will do, my daughter looks for shortcuts and variations. Why can't we just melt the butter first instead of using the mixer? she wonders. What if we add cocoa and make chocolate chocolate-chip oatmeal cookies? When this happens, it's not enough just to follow the steps. We have to think about why we mix the butter cold. We have to understand how the ingredients interact when heated or we won't know whether adding cocoa will improve the recipe or produce a culinary catastrophe.

Similarly, as long as we worship "the way we always have," there's not much urgency for discussing why and how we do things. But in times of rapid cultural change and experimentation (like ours), discussions become essential. We need to remind each other why we do what we do; we have to learn what the basic ingredients are and how they interact in order to make wise choices about potential changes.

That's an important part of what this series is about. One of the key disciplines of disciples is gathering for weekly worship. It shapes us in ways we don't even realize. So learning about worship together, thinking clearly about what we do in worship, and wondering how we can worship more deeply, is vital to our growth as disciples.

The first week of lessons in this series serves as an introduction to worship, outlining some important biblical and theological ingredients. The remaining four weeks are a step-by-step exploration of a fundamental pattern for worship—a beloved family worship recipe, if you will. You may recognize it in your own congregation's Sunday services. Along the way, alternating daily lessons explore several key adjectives that describe faithful worship—just as you can probably name some key adjectives that describe the qualities of desirable cookies: rich, chewy, sweet, and so on. These worship adjectives suggest virtues and values that no congregation would wish to do without.

The purpose here is not to define or defend some notion of correct or valid worship; it is rather to describe how beautifully, how meaningfully, how fully worship can express our love for God and God's love for us. It is less about correctness than completeness; less about legitimate worship and more about lavish worship—so that every week we can taste and see the goodness of the Lord.

Session 1
Party Planning

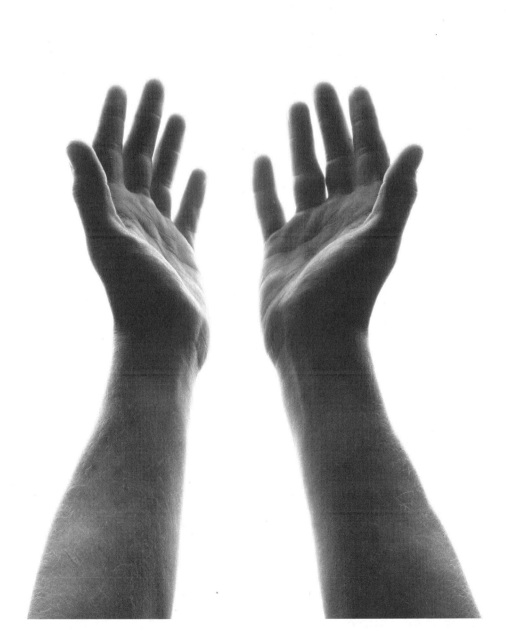

"Great" Worship 1

"I urge you, brothers and sisters, in view of God's mercy, to offer your bodies as a living sacrifice, holy and pleasing to God—this is true worship."

—Romans 12:1

Two worshipers were leaving the sanctuary after a particularly up-lifting service. The music was moving, the pastor had preached up a storm, and through the prayers and the rest of the service they felt deeply connected both with God and with their church community. "Wow," one remarked to the other, "we really *worshiped* today!"

Someone overhearing this conversation might wonder what they meant. There they were at church doing "churchy" things: praying, singing, listening to a sermon, giving their offerings—*of course* they worshiped. But it's not quite as simple as that.

Since the word *worship* can mean different things to different people, it may be helpful to sort out three common meanings as represented by the circles in the diagram on page 11.

First, all of life can be worship. The Reformed tradition places special emphasis on giving all our lives to God, no matter how or-dinary our lives seem. Worship isn't only something we do for an hour on the weekend. Our work, our play, all our common tasks—we seek to do them faithfully in gratitude for the grace we're given

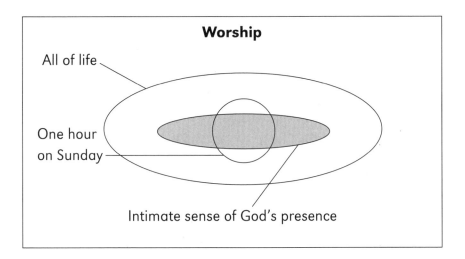

Worship

All of life

One hour on Sunday

Intimate sense of God's presence

in Jesus Christ. This is how we offer our bodies as sacrifices; this is our spiritual worship.

A second meaning of worship is the service of worship, the weekly assembly. In this sense, we might include not only the hour on Sunday, but a worship time on Wednesday evening, a wedding service, a funeral service. Used this way, worship refers to the sacred time we set aside to gather with other people of God. We perform actions (with our bodies)—singing, listening, speaking, praying aloud, kneeling, playing instruments, eating and drinking, washing—and in the very doing of them, we worship: we praise, adore, testify, confess, receive blessing. In worship we offer our actions to God and encounter God through them.

Finally, we use the word worship to refer to intimate experience of the divine. This may be what the worshiper we referred to earlier was getting at: she felt, in the worship service (the second meaning above) a sense of the power and presence of God. Perhaps you have had similar experiences in places other than church. You may have felt God's presence while hiking in the mountains or talking with a friend or praying in a quiet house. Sometimes these mystical experiences of awe or thanksgiving or comfort have an ecstatic character to them, as though we've been brought into God's very presence.

Of course, all these conceptions of worship are deeply interconnected. For instance, we long for worship in the third sense (of intimacy, even ecstasy) while we're at worship in the second sense (church). At its best, weekly worship makes space for deep connection with God to happen; something is wrong if it *never* does. But we can't engineer it through earnestness or technique. That's an alarmingly pagan, though not completely foreign, impulse (see 1 Kings 18). And even if we do not *feel* close to God at worship, it doesn't mean that God is absent from our weekly gathering.

In the end, the aim of good assembly-worship is to connect all three circles in a profound, God-glorifying way. Weekly worship creates the space and circumstances in which we encounter God powerfully, and through that encounter, God works to help us worship better on Tuesday and Wednesday and Thursday.

When someone says to me after a service, "That was great worship today, pastor!" I want to respond by saying something like this: Let's wait and see. After some months and years of this, let's see if the worship we offer to God in the gathered assembly glorifies God because we have been made better disciples, more loving and patient and kind and courageous. Let's see if our prayers and songs and sermons and offerings motivate us to bring this worship into the world where God is already at work. Let's see if what happened today helps us be better partners in the redemption Christ is bringing through the power of the Holy Spirit. Great worship? Let's see.

Think It Over

1. When have you had a strong experience of intimate worship lately? What was it about the circumstances that allowed God to work in you?

2. When have you worshiped in the third sense during a worship service (the second sense)? What combination of factors made God feel especially present to you?

In Other Words

"Christian worship is the worship of those who have died and risen again to a brand-new life and way of living. In this new community where Christ is head, things are different. Here people are less concerned with finding their life than with losing it for Christ. Here meekness, not muscle, is the mark of greatness."

—*Authentic Worship in a Changing Culture*

Live It Out

As you go about your activities today, choose a time when you are performing an ordinary task, and be especially attentive to how you might consider what you are doing as worship. The task might be something as simple as slicing an onion for the family dinner, preparing a presentation, or waiting at a stoplight. Perhaps performing the task in silence may help. As you work, offer what you are doing to God in prayer, as prayer.

By the Book (Worship Is Biblical) 2

"Your word is a lamp to my feet . . ."
—Psalm 119:105

In the dark days of late October, as the year dies, the early worship service at my church begins before the sun has fully risen. This past week, the sun broke over the treetops on the horizon right in the middle of the sermon, and a beautiful, bright orange glow filtered through the sanctuary windows, lighting up our whole worship space—the walls and the air and the people's faces.

It's a picture of how we want our worship to be: thoroughly *biblical,* suffused with the light of the Word of God. But what exactly does that mean? It may mean that we want our worship to feature the proclaimed Word of God in a sermon. But "biblical" worship is more than a meeting with a big chunk of preaching in it. Certainly that's a concentrated dose of light, and an important one. But the light of God's Word can shine in worship in many other ways too. Think of the ambient light that reaches us through the shape of the service, the themes we choose to focus on, the stories we tell, the biblical language that colors all we say and sing and pray.

Word Alert

Christian worship at its best is thoroughly *biblical*—guided by the Bible's instructions, shaped by its patterns, rooted in its truth, saturated with its language, following its narrative contours, and focusing on Jesus Christ.

We Protestants have always taken pride in our love of the Word and our dedication to doing all things in life biblically. However, visiting just a few worship services in a few Protestant congregations would be enough to demonstrate that what *biblical* means, as applied to worship, is not at all obvious.

A quick trip through a concordance won't do either. Does genuinely biblical worship involve offering sacrifices of animals or grains (Ex. 25-30)? A high priest entering a curtained holy place (Lev. 16; Heb. 13)? Renewing covenant vows (Josh. 24)? Singing loud praise (Ps. 96)? Reading and preaching from holy books (Neh. 8; Luke 4:16-21)? Small group prayer and fellowship (Acts 1:13-14)? A communal meal of remembrance and fellowship and hope (1 Cor. 11:20-22)?

If only the Bible were the instruction manual for Christian living we often wish it to be. If only it contained a detailed rulebook for worship in twenty-first-century North America. If it did, we could just check off the boxes and get it *right,* once and for all. But the Bible doesn't work like that. It's much more complex, much more flexible . . . and much more wonderful.

The Bible gives us all we need to discern how to worship in a way that is pleasing and acceptable to God. It does so by opening to us a rich treasure chest of stories, images, theological concepts, prayer language, and symbolic actions. All of these help us to know what God wants our worship (in all senses of the word) to be, and what God insists our worship should *not* be.

Our spiritually healthy impulse, then, to worship *biblically*—in both shape and content—is met in all sorts of faithful ways:

- Our worship is biblical as we follow biblical patterns for shaping time: yearly patterns (think of Advent and Easter); weekly patterns (six days and one day), and daily patterns that guide our Sunday worship (more on this later).

- Our worship is biblical as the words we say, the songs we sing, and the prayers we pray are saturated with the images, stories, and language of the Bible.

- Our worship is biblical as we follow Scripture's explicit instruction to pray and to praise, to confess and to testify, to wash and to eat in remembrance.

- Our worship is biblical as we read large chunks of Scripture when we meet together and when we attend carefully, through a preacher, to what God might be saying to us as individuals, as a church, as a society.

- Our worship is biblical as we retell and dramatically reenact the great sweeping story of God's love and find our own place in that story.

- Our worship is biblical when we place our central focus where the Bible does: on the person and work of Christ, and not on us.

Whatever confusion we may have about how these guidelines play out in our own congregations, we have this clarity and this comfort: acceptable worship of the living God happens on God's terms, not ours. We have every reason, then, to rejoice—since God's "terms" are the gracious covenant promises fulfilled in and through Jesus Christ.

Think It Over

1. What passage or story from the Bible do you recall from a recent worship service? When did it appear in the service? In a sermon? Children's message? Song? Prayer? As artwork in the sanctuary?

2. Can you imagine a worship service that was thoroughly biblical, but didn't use *any* words at all? What might it look like?

In Other Words

"There's a lovely Hasidic story of a rabbi who always told his people that if they studied the Torah, it would put Scripture on their hearts. One of them asked, 'Why *on* our hearts, and not *in* them?' The rabbi answered, 'Only God can put Scripture inside. But reading . . . can put it on your hearts, and then when your hearts break, the holy words will fall inside.'"

—Anne Lamott, *Plan B: Further Thoughts on Faith*

Live It Out

Sit quietly during your daily devotions. Instead of spending time reading or contemplating a particular passage of Scripture, be still and allow the Word of God already hidden in your heart (Ps. 119:11) to arise in your mind. Perhaps it is a verse you memorized long ago or a snippet from a song or a bit of a prayer. Rest in the light that Word brings to you.

Dance of Grace 3

"I pray . . . that all of them may be one, Father, just as you are in me and I am in you. May they also be in us so that the world may believe that you have sent me."
—John 17:20-21

My family has several crêches that we bring out at Christmastime and set up around the house. Once we've set all the little figures in place, though, my children like to go around messing up each other's scenes. Camels and sheep wander off, wise men ride on cows, and angels could turn up just about anywhere. Where should the angel go, anyway? There's no rule on that one!

Now imagine that you have a little scene of your own church at worship—a sanctuary crêche—with figures representing your pastor and everyone else, including you in your usual seat. But one figure is missing. Where might you place a figure representing God's presence? Of course, the second commandment cautions us against representing God with idols, but there is the baby Jesus in his manger in the Christmas crêche. So, just for the sake of this experiment (one designed to *combat* idolatry!)—where do you imagine God while you're at a worship service? In the front of the sanctuary? Floating above the communion table? Beside you in the pew? Inside the figures of the worshipers like a Russian nesting doll?

Although we know that God's presence is everywhere, this is a hard thing for us to get our minds around. Jeremy Begbie, a musician and theologian, offers a helpful analogy. He says that God's presence is like a three-tone chord: it fills every bit of our hearing, and no one tone of the chord has to get another tone to move over and make room. The tones *indwell* one another. They are distinct, yet sound together; they share the whole space without diminishing one another.

In this analogy, the three tones represent the three persons of the Trinity. One of the most distinctive mysteries of the Christian faith is the three-in-one nature of God. God exists in three persons, Father, Son, and Spirit, who indwell one another in an eternal, dynamic dance of self-giving love.

This beautiful and wondrous mystery has profound implications for our worship. For one thing, it means that if we think of God as being like the angel perched on the roof of the nativity stable —only "up there"—we misunderstand and limit God (another way of describing idolatry). God is not only *before us* to receive our praise and prayers, but God is *alongside* us in Jesus, perfecting our worship and presenting it to the Father (Heb. 4:4-10:10). Likewise, God is *within* us, in the Spirit, prompting our prayer (Rom. 8:26) and helping us to understand and to love and to obey the Word we hear from the Father (1 Cor. 2:12).

So when we worship, God is not a passive observer, waiting for us to sing louder or pray more earnestly before being present to us. God is active. God initiates worship—God created us to be worshiping creatures. It's part of the human DNA. God is the content and object of worship—it's all about God, not us. God enables our worship—prompting, perfecting, and receiving the worship we offer. The central active person in every aspect of worship is God.

This is immensely comforting. It means that we do not have to "perform" with excellent worship leadership or perfect attentiveness in order to make worship happen. Worship is all about grace. Jesus leads us into worship of the Father through the Spirit's power. As a worshiping community, we don't start something up on Sunday. Rather we are invited into the divine community of a triune God. Our role is to respond to the summons and join the dance.

Think It Over

1. It is sometimes said that different Christian denominations emphasize one person of the Trinity more than another. Pentecostals concentrate on the Holy Spirit, Presbyterians focus on the Father, while certain types of Evangelicals are all about Jesus. In your own prayer life, which member of the Trinity are you most conscious of? Do you imagine directing your prayers to a particular person of the Trinity, to all three at once, or perhaps (it's OK to admit it) to a vague divine entity?

2. Are there particular types of prayers you might direct to the Father, the Son, or the Spirit? What are some examples?

In Other Words

"Our God is the Father, Son, and Holy Spirit, who created us to participate in God's own Trinitarian *koinonia* [fellowship], and to live joyfully in that *koinonia* with one another in the church."

—Philip W. Butin, *The Trinity*

Live It Out

When you pray today—whether at private devotions or before meals or whenever—vary the way you name God. Here's one way to do that. Select an object you'll likely have with you all day, an object with component parts. Maybe that's a set of keys, or even the five fingers of your hand. For each key or finger, select a different name for God. You may wish to use some of the names from the list below. As you pray today, touch each part of your object, and say the corresponding name for God. Note whether anything changes in you or in your heart as you pray.

God the Father

Holy One (Ps. 71:22)
Judge of the earth (Ps. 94:2)
Fortress (Ps. 28:8)
God of all grace (1 Pet. 5:10)

God the Son

Teacher (John 13:13)
Bread of life (John 6:35)
True vine (John 15:1)
Our high priest (Heb. 5:10)

God the Spirit

Advocate (John 14:16)
Encourager (Acts 9:31)
Spirit of wisdom (Isa. 11:2)

Promises, Promises (Worship Is Covenantal)

4

> *"This is the covenant I will make with the house of Israel after that time, declares the LORD. I will put my law in their minds and write it on their hearts. I will be their God, and they will be my people."*
> —Jeremiah 31:33

> *"In the same way, after the supper he took the cup, saying, 'This cup is the new covenant in my blood. . . .'"*
> —Luke 22:20

When my family was traveling through England a few years ago, I noticed that the first architectural element we would usually encounter when we entered a cathedral was a baptismal font. These weren't portable bits of liturgical furniture—they were usually quite large, made of stone, and permanently set near the main entrance. This placement communicated that we all enter the church the same way—wet. We are able to approach God not because of anything *we* do, but because by God's grace we have been washed in the waters of baptism, the sign and seal of God's covenant with us. Whether or not we

---

Word Alert

A *font* is a water basin used for baptisms. While most of the fonts in our churches contain still water, the word font comes from the Latin word for fountain.

celebrate baptism on a given Sunday, we always come to worship as a people, to affirm and renew our covenantal relationship with the triune God.

Covenant—in both the Old and New Testaments—describes our relationship with God at its very essence. Again and again in the stories of the Bible, we see God making and renewing covenants: with Noah, with Abraham, with the children of Israel, with the exiled people. And then in a startling new form extending the covenant to us in the person of Jesus. They all are a little bit different, but the central biblical covenant is this divine declaration: "I will be your God, and you will be my people."

But a covenant is unlike the agreements we have with other people. We see in the Bible that God initiates covenants and then people respond. It is not an ar-

> **Word Alert**
>
> A *covenant* is a type of agreement between two parties: You do this and I'll do this.

rangement between equals but an act of amazing condescension and self-giving love. Perhaps most important, it is an act of *promise*. God promises to love, to forgive, to bless. We promise . . . well, we promise to faithfully receive those blessings. God's covenant with us is *not* a contract. In a contractual relationship, both sides must uphold the deal or the deal is off. In biblical covenants, God makes promises and then keeps them. God upholds the deal every time, even when the people involved fail repeatedly.

The closest thing to a covenant we have in modern life is a good marriage. We use covenant language for that relationship: we promise to love, honor, and cherish, no matter what—in sickness and health, in plenty and want. But it's hard not to think of marriage as a contract too. Especially in moments of conflict, we struggle to regard it as something greater than a mutually beneficial bargain we strike until it doesn't meet our needs anymore.

So when we gather for worship, we are responding to God's covenantal promises. We are affirming and *renewing* the covenant already made and sealed in our baptisms. We do this again and again because covenants are difficult for us to understand and to keep. Just as God frequently renews covenants with the people of God (see Josh. 24:1-28; 1 Kings 8:1-9:9; Ezra 9:1-10:19), so God renews the divine covenant with us every week.

In fact, one helpful way of understanding our weekly worship is to see it as an extended covenantal conversation between God and us, modeled after the ones mentioned above: God speaks, we respond; we speak, God responds. And since this is a covenant made not with us as individuals, but as a *people*, sometimes we speak to each other, marveling over God's faithfulness or encouraging one another. Covenantal relationships are based on promises, forgiveness, and faithfulness. We can never fully uphold our end of the deal with God, yet God is always faithful.

Think It Over

1. What relationships in your life would you consider covenantal? In what specific ways do you renew that covenant? For example, you might renew your marriage covenant by going on a weekly date or your commitment to a friend by honoring his or her confidences.

2. List some ways that God speaks in your congregation's worship services. List some ways the people respond to God.

In Other Words

"The relationship that God welcomes us into [in worship] is not a contractual relationship of obligations but a promise-based or covenantal relationship of self-giving love."

—*The Worship Sourcebook*

Live It Out

There is a famous story that Martin Luther enjoyed walking in the rain. He enjoyed letting the water douse him as he remembered that in his baptism he was joined to the life, death, and resurrection of Jesus Christ. This week, every time you get wet—in the shower, in the rain, as you wash your hands—take the opportunity to remember the covenant promises God makes in your baptism: to forgive your sin, to fill you with the Holy Spirit, and to unite you to Jesus and to his body, the church.

Baseball/ Complexity 5

*"What then shall we say, brothers and sisters?
When you come together, each of you has a hymn, or
a word of instruction, a revelation, a tongue or
an interpretation. Everything must be done so
that the church may be built up. . . . But everything
should be done in a fitting and orderly way."*
—1 Corinthians 14:26, 40

If you were to ask a serious baseball fan to describe the essence
of baseball, what do you suppose that person might say? What is
the heart of the game? Perhaps this fan would speak passionately
about the contest of will and skill between pitcher and batter,
or of the ballet of catching, leaping, and throwing as fielders
make a double play, or of the elegant interplay of statistics in the
manager's mind, or of the roar of the crowd when a batter hits a
homerun on a 3-2 count with the bases loaded, or of the moment
when a father turns to his son and predicts what the next pitch
will be, and to the son's amazement, he's right.

No doubt if you were to ask several baseball fans, you would get
several different answers. Baseball is a complex "social practice"—
a kind of ritual activity with rules and traditions, rich with delights
and meanings beyond itself. It can't really be reduced to a single
essence. In fact, if you think about it, you notice that any one of

those beloved moments of the game could not possibly have its full meaning without all the other aspects of the game creating the context.

Thinking about the complexity of baseball helps us recognize that worship is similarly complex—far more so, of course, because worship is an interaction with God. You may have heard people express a longing to "get to the heart of worship." Maybe you've even felt that impulse yourself. But what is the heart of worship? Is it a certain kind of encounter with God? Is it a certain biblical order of worship, or a certain kind of preaching? Is it an intimate experience of prayer or song?

This desire to find the heart of worship is understandable. We often try to cope with complex things by finding a simple truth or essence. And perhaps you have experienced how secondary things in worship—perhaps certain technologies or music styles or architectural features—can inappropriately take on primary importance. When that happens we go looking for that essence to set priorities straight.

But perhaps we ought to have a little more patience with and even delight in the complexity of worship. Good worship will necessarily do many things at once. It warns, encourages, reminds, inspires, and unites us; it delights and glorifies God. No doubt you could think of many other things worship does. Are any of these more important than the others? Does any one get at the "heart" of worship? Could any happen without the others?

When I do workshops, I sometimes lead groups into a worship space and ask participants to choose what they think is the most important place in the sanctuary, the place that represents the heart of worship, and to stand there. Then we talk about our choices. Some stand next to the pulpit and mention the centrality of preaching. Others encircle the communion table and talk about Christ's body at the Lord's Supper. Some locate the central instrument—the piano or organ or drumset—and talk about the joy of praising God. Some sit in the pews and say that people are the most important elements in worship; others stand in the doorway and speak about evangelism.

As we talk about our choices, we all recognize the value in what the others say. We see that *every* choice is a good one. And we experience the richness of standing in a number of different places to look around and to remind each other, "This is what happens here, and here's why it's so important." In a sense, that's exactly what we'll be doing for the next weeks in this study.

Think It Over

1. Consider these six activities: a lecture, a pep rally, a music concert, a theatrical production, a date, an AA meeting. Which is worship *most* like?

   As you think through each comparison, try to imagine both positive and negative features. So, for example, worship can be like a lecture in that we go in order to gain wisdom from someone whose opinion we trust (such as the pastor). On the other hand, a bad lecture can become dull. Make notes on some of your thoughts.

2. Does your congregation come to worship with expectations they bring, perhaps unknowingly, from any of these other cultural activities? How might that help or harm their ability to participate in worship?

In Other Words

"God's people gather in cathedrals and in straw huts, in store-fronts and in underground houses. Musical instruments and the sounds and songs they produce vary greatly around the world and through the ages. The fact is that God is honored and worshiped in a multitude of different ways."

—*Authentic Worship in a Changing Culture*

Live It Out

Someone might say that the heart of baseball—in all its complexity—could be summarized as simply being at or in the game—being really *present* to all that happens there. If there is any truth in this, might we also say that the complex essence of worship (whether Sunday services or intimate encounters or all-of-life) is to be fully *present* to God? Today, grab a sticky note or maybe one of those rubber bracelets—the kind that you find everywhere reminding people to "live strong" or fight AIDS. Get a Sharpie and write "God is here." Then put it in a prominent place: the fridge, a mirror, your dashboard; or wear it on your wrist. Every time you look at it, practice living that moment fully in the presence of the omnipresent, triune God.

Party Planning
Discussion Guide

My wife and I are planning a small party. We've already invited some good friends, and we've reserved the date on our calendar. Though we don't spend as much time with them as we'd like, it will be wonderful to get together and to reconnect. Here's the problem: the evening is going to involve some tough choices. What should we do? Sit in the living room and share stories about the good old days? Talk about the latest good book we've read? Ask each other for advice about difficult things in our lives—family and money and work? Delight together in good music, maybe even get some instruments out? How much time should we set aside for each activity? What is most important? Do we plan carefully or play it by ear?

Though we have lots of choices, I'm pretty certain there are a few non-negotiables. We'll be intentional about saying hello and saying goodbye. And in between, we'll do two things for sure: we'll talk and we'll eat. There is a basic pattern here, an age-old wisdom that we've inherited and learned to trust. We gather, talk, eat, leave. Each is important, each needs attention. It's a pattern some have compared with a fundamental structure for worship.

As you might guess, the Church, diverse as it is, has come up with a dizzying array of solutions to the problem of how to select and arrange the elements of a worship service. How do we worship in a way that takes into account all we've talked about already: worship that

- attends to Scripture's instructions,
- pursues all of worship's complex goals,

- engages the triune God in revelation and response,
- renews the covenant of grace,
- glorifies God,
- and molds us into greater Christ-likeness for all-of-life worship?

Since the Bible does not dictate a particular order of worship, the church has felt relatively free to experiment. (This freedom has been exercised in some historical periods more than in others). Yet amidst the experimentation and diversity, the church has either retained or rediscovered a surprising unanimity that stretches across cultures and denominations and centuries, and is expressed in what is known as the classic four-fold *ordo*.

> **Word Alert**
>
> **Ordo is a Latin word meaning "order" or "structure." It refers to the meaning-filled pattern into which the elements of worship are arranged.**

At its heart, the four-fold *ordo* is a celebratory congregational encounter with Jesus Christ. It focuses on two nonnegotiable and holy things: a *book* and a *meal*. The practices surrounding both are rooted in Scripture and are part of the early church's Jewish inheritance. The first-century synagogue service focused on hearing God's *Word* read and explained (see Luke 4:16-30). Jewish worship life in the home focused on prayers of thanksgiving and a *meal* actively remembering God's saving acts (the Passover) and sealing God's promises. These two activities are anticipated by the *gathering,* and extended into all-of-life worship as the people are *sent out.*

These, then, are the contours of the fourfold pattern:

- *Gathering*—the congregation of God's people
- *Book*—the proclamation of the Word
- *Meal*—the celebration at the Table
- *Sending*—the dispersion of the Church into the world

We will spend the next weeks studying these four movements of worship. And today we will see how this pattern emerges, in part at least, from a key New Testament story about an encounter between Jesus and some of his disciples.

Ice Breakers
(15 minutes—give or take)

If this is a new group meeting for the first time, **take some time to get acquainted**. Distribute blank 3 x 5 cards and write down in bullet form five things about yourself that you don't mind others knowing about you. Have one person collect the cards and read them out loud to see if the group can guess who each card belongs to. Don't worry if you're new to the group—there's no winning or losing. The more you get to know each other, the more everybody wins.

Options
If that seems too gimmicky, just go around the circle and introduce yourselves. Include a brief, fun story of when you did something you really wished you hadn't done.

If this is a continuing group, take a few minutes to regroup. **If there are any new members, everyone should briefly introduce themselves as in the option above.** If not, invite group members to share a memory of a time when they felt deeply connected to God in worship. Was it while singing a beloved hymn with God's people during a Sunday service? Celebrating the Lord's Supper? Observing God's glory on a starry night? How did you feel? Take some time to share what it was that made this particular worship experience so memorable.

For Starters

(10 minutes)

Think about the way your own congregation structures its worship services. What does this tell you about what it considers most important? Can you identify what part feels like the dramatic "high point" of your weekly worship? What is the moment that the agenda builds toward and falls away from afterward? Where does your congregation pour most of its resources in time and energy?

What does the selected high point say about the purpose of worship and the relationship between God and humans?

Let's Focus

(5 minutes)

Read the introduction to this session; then have someone read this focus statement aloud:

Luke 24 tells the story of two disciples who have a life-changing encounter with the risen Jesus. The story isn't just about other people—it is *our* story. One of the disciples is Cleopas, the other remains unnamed, an empty silhouette that we fill with our own features, our own hopes, our own disappointments.

Think of Luke's story as the script for every weekly Christian worship service:

- Disciples walk along a road colored by sorrow and dashed hopes. Jesus meets them where they are.

- Responding to their despair, Jesus explains to them the Scriptures, telling them the sweeping story of God's salvation.

- This lights a fire in the disciples' hearts that they only sense fully when they share a meal together and recognize Jesus' presence in the breaking of the covenantal bread.

- Full of courage and delight, they rush away to share their good news with others.

These four movements—gathering, word, meal, sending—correspond to the fourfold structure of worship that so many churches use to shape their own communal gatherings.

Word Search

(20 minutes)

Many have seen the account in Luke 24 of Jesus' post-resurrection appearance to the disciples on the road to Emmaus as a model for the fourfold structure of the Church's worship. **Read aloud the following Scripture passages and briefly discuss at least some of the questions under each one (or formulate better ones of your own).**

- Luke 24:13-24
  Cleopas and his friend were on a journey. In what way are you on a journey too?

  What was the emotional state of the travelers? Do you ever come to worship feeling like they did?

  Who initiates the contact between Jesus and the disciples?

  What kept the two disciples from recognizing Jesus?

  How is the "gathering" portion of your worship service like the encounter described in these verses?

- Luke 24:25-27
  What parts of Scripture do you imagine Jesus explained to the disciples?

  What was the theme of Jesus' sermon? Should it be the underlying theme of each sermon?

In what ways does the "book" portion of your congregation's worship resemble the encounter described in these verses?

- Luke 24:28-32
  Jesus doesn't insist, doesn't force himself on us, doesn't bowl us over with incontrovertible evidence of his reality. He awaits an invitation, and then he accepts. How do we invite Jesus to our meals?

Consider the verbs used to describe Jesus' actions with the bread: *took, gave thanks* (blessed), *broke,* and *gave*. What other scriptural meal do these remind you of? Do you do each of these four things at your Lord's Supper celebrations?

The disciples don't work extra hard in order to recognize Jesus—the text says their "eyes were opened." What role do you think their hearing of Scripture had on their ability in this moment to see what was right in front of them?

In what ways does the "meal" portion of your congregation's worship resemble the encounter described in these verses?

- Luke 24:33-35
  Jesus is present and then mysteriously absent. But this doesn't discourage the disciples. They were immediately energized to return to Jerusalem. Does the meal energize you? In what way?

Do the disciples seem transformed by their encounter with Jesus?

The disciples are eager to tell others about their encounter with Jesus. When has an experience been so powerful for you that you have been energized to tell others about it right away?

In what ways does the "sending" portion of your congregation's worship resemble what is described in these verses?

Bring It Home

(15 minutes, or as time allows)

Choose one of the following options:

Option 1

Imagine that you're a committee in charge of planning a worship service. You're given a blank slate and told you can do anything you want. **Decide what will be part of your new worship service.** Scripture reading? Prayers for healing? An offering? A time of community singing? Silent meditation? Announcements? The Lord's Supper? A movie clip? Confession? Preaching? Drama? Testimony? A litany of thanksgiving? Once you've decided what's on the list and what's not, how will you decide what goes first, second, third and so on? How much time will each element get? What are the most important parts?

Option 2

Discuss the following questions with the group:

- Take a typical weekly worship service in your church (it may or may not be written down). Identify how each element of worship fits the fourfold *ordo* we've been looking at. Are there any elements that do not fit?

- Discuss together whether you think the meal (Lord's Supper) is important at each worship service. Keep in mind that you do not need to come to agreement, but do listen to each other's views.

Option 3

In a small group, select one moment in the four sections of the Luke 24 passage (see Word Search), that exemplifies the fourfold

ordo. Take five minutes to discuss the section you've chosen, and then act it out. Do it as worshipfully as possible, without using any words.

Pray It Through
(10 minutes)

Divide your prayer time into four sections of roughly two minutes each. Have the prayer leader begin each section of the prayer by reading the words below. The group may then pray, either aloud or in silence, their joys or concerns as prompted by the passage.

1. "He asked them, 'What are you discussing together as you walk along?' They stood still, their faces downcast."

2. "He explained to them what was said in all the Scriptures."

3. "He took bread, gave thanks, broke it and began to give it to them. Then their eyes were opened and they recognized him."

4. "They got up and returned at once to Jerusalem."

Live It Out
(10 minutes)

At the next worship service you attend try to have the *ordo* we've discussed today in mind. See if you can trace it through the service. Also think about your worship in view of some of the other aspects of worship you've read this week. How is God the initiator and helper, as well as the one being worshiped? How is this expressed in worship? In what ways is the worship service a kind of reenactment of the covenant between God and his people?

Web Alert

Be sure to check out the participants' section for this session on our website, www.GrowDisciples.org, for interesting links and suggestions for readings and activities that will deepen your understanding of worship.

Session 2
Assembling the Assembly (Gathering)

First Impressions 1

"Come, let us sing for joy to the LORD;
let us shout aloud to the Rock of our salvation.
Let us come before him with thanksgiving
and extol him with music and song."

Psalm 95:1-2

Years ago, my family belonged to a church whose pastor, Norm, believed in the importance of first impressions. So he began every worship service by stepping to the baptismal font at the front of the sanctuary. While pouring water into it, he would say: "We gather here today as God's forgiven people. And the sign of that forgiveness is the water of baptism."

This pastor found a wise and joyful way to remind us every week that we come to worship *because God invites us*. We do not come out of our own strength of will or lifestyle preference or spiritual virtue. We don't come out of guilt or fear; we don't come to get something from God or even to get our spiritual batteries recharged. Even if these motivations are sometimes at work in us— and they are—beneath them all is the truth that we come because God calls us. The word used in the New Testament for the church— *ekklesia*—means "called-out ones."

Beginning our worship by letting God have the first word—often called a "call to worship"—and then responding in gratitude sets a healthy conversational pattern. It also sets a joyful, expectant, prayerful tone for the rest of worship. What does it mean to let God have the first word?

There are many ways to do this well. Pastor Norm reminded us of baptism as the sign of God's grace, freely given to us. Other churches offer a word of blessing from Scripture: "Grace and peace to you from God our Father and the Lord Jesus Christ" (Phil. 1:2), or a choral "call to worship" with lyrics drawn from the Psalms. I know of one congregation that reminds itself why they gather with a song they pray each week: "The Lord of heaven and earth be worshiped in this place, the covenant of grace be renewed."

I have also been to worship services in which a pastor or other leader begins worship by saying something like this: "Hello, it's great to have you here today! Thanks for coming!" Some congregational announcements might follow, and then some songs declaring God's goodness. Beginning a service this way seems warm and friendly. The leader helps to make people feel welcome, and that's a worthwhile thing to do. But I always feel as if something is missing. When we begin worship that way, we are making good horizontal connections to each other, but not vertical ones. God seems more like an observer than the One who calls us to worship.

By contrast, when we begin worship with words of Scripture or in some other way acknowledge that God acts first—moving us by the Spirit to our worship—we set the tone for everything that comes after. Then it's

Word Alert

If we consider worship a conversation between God and the congregation, *horizontal connections* take place whenever the conversation flows among the people of God, and *vertical connections* take place whenever the conversation flows from God to the people or from the people to God.

good to welcome one another—remembering that God welcomes us first and forms us into the body of Christ.

Think It Over

1. How does the worship service begin in your church? Is there a sense of the vertical and horizontal dimensions of worship?

2. Does God get the first word?

In Other Words

"The call to worship . . . must acknowledge loudly and clearly that many things call to us for our worship, but it is God alone to whom we ultimately bow."

—Lisa Nichols Hickman, *The Worshiping Life*

Live It Out

Pay special attention today to first impressions: the first few minutes of a meeting, the first thirty seconds of your interaction with someone you meet for the first time, the first minutes of the day. Do whatever you can to help those first impressions be good ones.

The Participate-o-meter (Worship Is Participative) 2

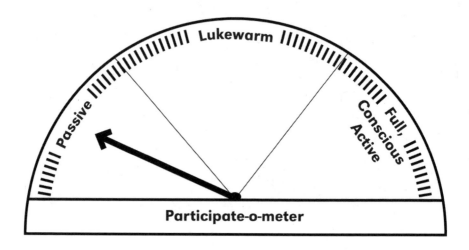

"*Ezra praised the LORD, the great God; and all the people lifted their hands and responded, 'Amen! Amen!' Then they bowed down and worshiped the Lord with their faces to the ground.*"

—Nehemiah 8:6

I used to work with college students to plan and lead campus worship services. One way we would assess the effectiveness of a certain part of the service (a song or drama, for example) was by asking, "What did the participate-o-meter register?" If the congregation mumbled, if their eyes glazed over, if they looked at their watches regularly, then the meter gave a little twitch and was still.

But if the congregation sang with full voice, if they sat on the edge of their seats during the sermon or testimony, if there was silence during prayer as vivid as the singing—then we knew the partici-pate-o-meter was bouncing high on the scale. And that was where we wanted it, of course. Good worship, led hospitably, engages the congregation so that they are not just present in the room, but fully present to God.

My two sisters are actors. They tell me that the same sort of intui-tive "participate-o-meter" is often used by people in theater to measure whether the audience was fully present to the evening's performance. This is an interesting comparison. If you remember, last week we wondered how a worship service might be compared to a drama or a play. Someone in your group may have noticed that those who lead worship sometimes appear to be *performing* for a congregation/audience. And sometimes that audience is a rather passive one, content to watch "the show."

The Danish thinker Søren Kirkegaard suggested that this picture is badly mistaken. He argued that worshipers ought to consider themselves the *actors* in worship and God as the *audience*. In that analogy, those who lead worship are simply the stagehands, whis-pering to the congregation from backstage: "OK, here's where you say, "Amen! Jesus is Lord!"

The point is this: worship is *participative*. It's the role of leaders to both encourage and enable the full, conscious, and active partici-pation of the congregation. And it's the role of the congregation to participate actively.

We see it in Nehemiah: the worshipers call out; they lift their hands; they bow down. The same chapter notes that during the reading of God's Word, interpreters were there to be certain the people *understood* it.

A recent worship document uses the rich phrase "full, conscious, and active" to describe the participation of God's people in worship. That's our goal: we are to participate fully in worship—all the time, and with all of our heart, mind, soul, and strength. This means leaders are to think of their role in terms of hospitality. They need to ask, How can we lead the congregation sensitively and comfortably, while also challenging them toward the goal of full, conscious, active participation?

The trick with the participate-o-meter is that it's hard to "read" a congregation. Spiritual participation has mental, emotional, and physical components, and it can look different for different people. When my grandpa sat stock-still, his eyes welling with tears as he sang "For All the Saints," he was participating as fully and actively and consciously as the college students I worked with who bounced up and down and pumped their fists in the air as they sang "Shout to the Lord." Sadly, differences like these have sometimes led to divided churches.

Our participation in worship takes place *within the congregation*. Whenever there are some among us who are unable to participate fully in worship—for whatever reason—it diminishes *everyone's* ability to worship fully. My wife and I have noticed over the years that when our small children are bored and nonparticipative, counting ceiling lights or poking each other, we have found it difficult to worship attentively.

But participation has a wonderful cyclical effect in the other direction too. Attentive participation among some invites others to join. So as my children have grown, they are more able to sing, read, listen, pray, watch, eat, and drink. And now we worship better ourselves. Fully. Consciously. Actively. With them and with the whole congregation.

Think It Over

1. When does your congregation seem most eager to participate? Are they great singers of hymns? Wonderful listeners and responders to sermons? Skilled at moving their bodies to the music?

2. Are there times when the participate-o-meter seems not to register much? What do you think might help?

In Other Words

"[O]ur liturgical life must witness to the Priesthood of all Believers. Worship is never the task of a special class, to be performed by them while the congregation simply sits and watches."

—Howard Hagemann, *Pulpit and Table*

Live It Out

Actively prepare to participate in worship this week. Read the Scripture text ahead of time. Pray that people will be ready to worship together. Ask the people in your household to prepare for Sunday by tidying up, planning the Sunday meals, laying out clothes, or whatever else will make you less distracted when Sunday morning comes.

Yay, God! 3

"Let everything that has breath praise the LORD.
Praise the LORD."
—Psalm 150:6

Some friends of mine have a little girl who recently turned two years old. They have been teaching her to pray before meals since she could sit up in a high chair. Before she eats, she folds her hands, closes her eyes, bows her head, and waits while mommy or daddy says some words. Then, to conclude the prayer, she opens her eyes and raises her arms over her head while mom or dad exclaims, "Yay, God!"

In this simple and delightful way, my friends are teaching their tiny daughter to praise. She loves this ritual, and if for some reason her parents forget to go through with it, she will fold her hands without touching her food and plead, "Pway? Pway? Pway?"

We praise in worship because we have been taught to do so. We praise in worship because the Bible commands it. But more than that, we praise in worship because when we encounter God, it is the right way to respond. Worship begins with God calling us to worship, inviting us to gather in his presence. And in response, we praise.

There are at least two component parts to our praise (there may be more, but this is a start). The first is *adoration,* where we speak directly *to* God, expressing our awe, submission, honor, reverence, and love. We do this with our words or with our songs, with our bodies, and sometimes perhaps more fitting, with our adoring silence. When the Bible speaks about people bowing down or kneeling, when my friends' daughter bows her head, this is praise as adoration.

The second part of praise is *celebration*—where we speak either to God or to each other, acknowledging who God is and celebrating the mighty deeds God has done and is still doing in our world. Yay, God!

In our praise, we do more than bow and say "Yay." We ground our praise in who God is and what God has done—in God's *attributes* and *actions.* So, for example, we address God with names that say something about God: You are mighty, holy, just, merciful, loving, gracious. . . . And we speak to God and to each other about God's actions: You created us; you guarded Daniel in the lion's den; you sent Jesus to die for us; you formed the church by your Spirit; you sustain your creation; you shield us from final evil; you forgive us; you make us more honest and loving and holy. Praise helps us to worship not some distant, passive, abstract notion of divinity but the living God of David, Mary Magdalene, and Saint Paul.

Yet all this hardly captures the deep *joy* of praising our God. Even though we are commanded to praise whether or not we feel like it, the language of praise both expresses and calls forth from us joyful feelings.

Those feelings are often connected with the language of music. For many people *musical* praise is such a central part of worship they hardly think about worship as anything else. Whether with organs or choirs or praise bands, with a cappella singing or a circle of djembes, many of us cannot imagine surviving long without musical praise. Our spirits would wither. Indeed, the people of God have combined words of praise with music since ancient times. The Psalms often call for using instruments to praise God.

Of course, music is not the *only* way we express praise. David and Miriam danced their praise. Joshua and the angels shouted theirs. You might say that Rembrandt painted his and John Calvin preached his. There are as many ways to praise as there are people, and there are particular ways of praise that are unique only to you.

> (Word Alert)
>
> A *djembe* (pronounced *jen bay*) is a skin-covered hand drum shaped like a large goblet and meant to be played with bare hands. According to the Bamana people in Mali, the name of the djembe comes directly from the saying "Anke dje, anke be" which literally means "everyone gather together."

Of course, God doesn't need our praise, but we do need to praise God. Praise inoculates us against cynicism and despair in a world that is often hard and cold. Praise helps us to combat idolatry. Praise helps us put the wonders of this world into God's account, as it were. Every time we say "Praise God from whom all blessings flow!" we are saying that blessings do not flow from our hard work, or from the stock market, or from sparkling white teeth. Praise helps us map our joys, our experiences of awe and thanksgiving—our very existence—to its genuine source, the Creator. Praise also helps us, even in our deepest sorrows, to remember that nothing can separate us from the love of God.

Little Althea, my friends' child, is learning a language for joy even before she has many words. Our acts of praise in worship teach us a language we can't learn very well anywhere else.

Think It Over

1. Can you recall a time when your praise, spoken or sung with the congregation, was especially meaningful for you? Was there something you were particularly joyful or thankful about?

2. Can you recall a time when you were sorrowful or grieving, and praise felt like a balm?

3. Can you think of a time when you seemed so distant from God that praise felt empty to you?

In Other Words

"The Bible commands us to worship and praise, not because God is an egoist who loves flattery but so that we might not be left without a language for joy."

—Debra Rienstra, *So Much More*

Live It Out

Watch television for twenty minutes or get a magazine and look at all the pictures of joyful people. Notice what message is being sent about the source of that joy. Is it a new car? A rising portfolio? A beautiful scene in nature? These are *powerful* images that tempt us to unwitting idolatry. Fight it by cutting the pictures out (or doing so in your mind) and saying, "Praise God, not _____."

All of Me (Worship Is Holistic) 4

"'Love the Lord your God with all your heart and with all your soul and with all your strength and with all your mind."

—Luke 10:27

Our children love playing soccer, and over the past few years my wife and I have spent many wonderful hours at their games. We find this great fun. We jump up and cheer when they do well; we groan in dismay when the other team scores. We strategize about free kicks and analyze how many tournament points the team needs to go the finals. We talk with the other parents and grand-parents at halftime or kick the ball around on the sideline with younger soccer siblings.

Soccer is hardly the most important thing in our lives. Still, it's fair to say that we really get into it. We join with all the others there and bring our whole selves to the sport: thoughts, feelings, our bodies—*everything*.

How wonderful then, that something similar happens with an activity so much more central to our lives: worship. How wonderful when we join others and bring all our selves to worship—body and soul, mind and heart, doubt and belief, lament and joy—to our encounter with God. The best worship helps congregations do exactly this. It is *holistic*; that is to say, it engages our minds, our hearts, our bodies, our spirits—our very essence—for in worship the Holy Spirit can transform our very essence.

But probably all of us feel, at least sometimes, that our whole selves are not very involved in worship.

- Maybe there are habits or character flaws we want to hide because we believe they are too shameful to bring before God or God's people. That's why the best worship will provide an explicit confession of sin and a bold assurance of God's forgiveness and healing.

- Maybe it seems like we're too young or too old to participate fully in worship, or maybe some of the things we do in worship leave the older and younger members of the congregation out of the picture. That's why the best worship will include the songs of both the young and old, and will make use of familiar patterns and broad gestures so that those who cannot understand or hear the words can still know what is going on.

- Maybe there are days we have doubts about whether God cares about us, or we're carrying a heavy burden of grief and it feels like there's no room for our shadows in a service full of joy and light. That's why the best worship will make room for the full range of human emotion—where we can express and God can embrace not only the joy of Psalm 103 ("Praise the LORD, my soul") but also the despair of Psalm 42 ("Why, my soul, are you downcast?").

- Maybe our church's worship feels so brainy and wordy that we are engaged only from the neck up, and we are so stationary during the service that it seems we might as well leave our bodies at home. That's why the best worship will not only stimulate our minds but will also make room for visual communication and movement, knowing that beauty to touch our souls comes from God, and that we learn about God's grace in our *bodies* by standing and sitting, kneeling and swaying, dancing and singing, eating, drinking, and washing.

It's tough to make space in worship for all our complexities as individuals and as congregations. Yet it's a goal worth pursuing, because we know that we need the transforming power of God to touch us—every part of us, and every one of us.

Think It Over

1. What parts of you come easily to worship? What parts of you hide in worship?

2. What could you do to bring more of yourself to worship?

3. What might you change about how your congregation worships in order to make it more holistic?

In Other Words

"Holiness has most often been revealed to me in the exquisite pun of the first syllable, in holes—in not enough help, in brokenness, mess."

—Anne Lamott, *Plan B: Further Thoughts on Faith*

Live It Out

The Reformed tradition has always had a special appreciation for the Psalms, which, as the church has long recognized, model for us the full range of human experience. Choose a few verses from a psalm today and memorize them. Try to choose some verses that express an emotion that you don't find easy to express in worship.

If you're artistically inclined, spend a few minutes trying to sketch a picture of those verses. If you're more into movement, imagine how you might hold your body in order to speak these verses from the Psalms. If you want, take that posture and pray those verses. Notice how your thoughts and feelings and will are shaped by your body's posture.

The Penitential Parabola 5

"If we claim to be without sin, we deceive ourselves and the truth is not in us. If we confess our sins, he is faithful and just and will forgive us our sins and purify us from all unrighteousness."

—1 John 1:8-9

There is a ritual practiced regularly—if not particularly well—at my home. I'll bet it's familiar to you too. It goes something like this (though the names and circumstances change each time):

"Jacob, did you mean to thwack Philip in the head with your light saber?"

(Sullenly) "Not really."

"But you did it, right?"

"Yeah."

"Do you think you should say something to him?"

"I suppose. But *he* was—"

"We'll get to him in a minute. What do *you* want to say about what *you* did?"

(Quickly and woodenly) "I'm sorrmrmumblemumble."

"OK, that's a start. Now tell Philip—what are you sorry *for*?"

(More clearly) "Philip, I'm sorry I konked you in the head."

"Good. Now, Philip: Did you *believe* that apology? Do you accept it?"

"Well, it wasn't very good—but yes. I guess."

One of the most important habits we learn as we grow older is how to apologize. It doesn't come naturally, nor does it come easily. But we can't have healthy relationships unless we're willing to clean out the junk that gets in the way when we hurt or offend each other. We have to admit that we've messed up and ask for forgiveness.

The Bible teaches us the importance of the discipline of confession for our spiritual hygiene. We see it, for example, in Jesus' story of the Pharisee and the tax collector who go to the temple to pray. The one who began his prayer by saying "I'm not worthy" is the one whose prayer was heard and who went home justified. This cleaning isn't something *we* do—*God* does it. But God invites us to cooperate in the process by regularly recognizing our "junk," confessing it, and hearing God's word of grace and cleansing and forgiveness.

Many churches practice this important spiritual habit during worship. Some may sing a song of confession such as "Change My Heart, O God." Others may recite aloud together a prayer of confession: "We confess that we have sinned by what we have done and by what we have left undone." Others may use a litany, perhaps one that incorporates Psalm 51 or 130 or some other Scripture. Still others may participate in a time of silence inter- spersed with the Greek prayer *Kyrie Eleison,* which means "Lord, have mercy."

Often our confession recognizes that sin is not merely the sum total of individual trespasses. Sin can be systemic—we can sin as a community in our institutions or in practices that hurt others, even if we don't mean to. So sometimes the confession is articulated as more of a lament at the world's brokenness and our part in it: "I am messed up" and "We've messed up" as well as "I messed up." Even when we say these words half-mumbling (as we sometimes do), saying them is an important part of growing into meaning them more deeply.

That's why confession is such an important part of the worship service. Everyone carries around junk. In church, we give that junk a name, and we bring it to the One who can relieve us of it fully and forever.

After the time of confession, a pastor or leader offers a word of assurance, usually from Scripture, that God will keep the promise to forgive us: "As far as the east is from the west, so far has he removed our transgressions from us" (Ps. 103:12). It's a movement downward into awareness of sin and then upward into forgiveness and reconciliation: a penitential parabola.

> **Word Alert**
>
> The *parabola* is an important concept in abstract mathematics, but it also has many practical applications in engineering, physics—and, who knew, worship! It looks like this:

Of course, the pastor or leader who pronounces forgiveness is not the one who forgives. He or she only reminds us of a promise that comes from God through the work of Christ, as testified in the Scriptures. In fact, "we have confidence to enter the Most Holy Place" (Heb. 10:19) because of what Jesus has already done.

We can only come to God for forgiveness because—like the father who runs out to meet his prodigal son and embraces him before he can even speak—God *first* offers us a divine and all-embracing compassion that overwhelms all our sin.

Think It Over

What kind of junk are you carrying around inside you? Think not only about particular thoughts and deeds that you have committed, but about deep character flaws or wounds that you need to let God heal. Let the Spirit reveal these things to you.

In Other Words

"We're no damn good, but God loves us anyway."

—Billy Campbell, *Brother to a Dragonfly*

Live It Out

Do some cleaning today—really: do the dishes, dust a room, empty out a closet. As you clean, ask God to clean out your soul. Confess where you are dusty or grimy or moldy, and imagine the Holy Spirit making you clean.

Assembling the Assembly
Discussion Guide

I have some friends who never come to church on time. They deliberately arrive ten minutes late on Sunday morning so that they can skip what they call the "opening exercises." I'm not sure if they find the music of the opening praise sequence not to their taste, or whether they don't like confessing their sin, or whether they are uncomfortable as the congregation greets one another in Christ's name. They think that what happens in the first ten or fifteen minutes of worship is superfluous, boring, unimportant. The sermon is what counts, they figure; skipping the opening is no big deal.

But it *is* a big deal, because they are missing out on some of the most formative parts of our corporate worship, parts that communicate so much about who God is and why we've assembled. As we learned this week, the first things that happen when the church gathers set the tone for everything else that follows.

Last week we looked at some basic definitions of worship and we considered the wisdom of the four-fold structure *(ordo)* that gives shape to weekly worship services for many churches: Gathering, Word, Meal, Sending.

This week we looked at the elements of worship that take place during the Gathering time, often at the beginning of the service. We thought about how God calls us to gather for worship and speaks the first word in our covenantal conversation. We discussed praise—in celebration and adoration—as the language of joy, the natural response to who God is and what God has done for us. And we pondered the penitential parabola by which we confess our sin and hear God's Word of gracious forgiveness. We also noted how worship invites our full, conscious, active participation.

Isaiah 6 bears witness to Isaiah's encounter with our mighty and holy God. We see in that encounter many of the same pieces we've been discussing: an awareness of God's presence, praise for who God is, a confession of sin, and an act of forgiveness.

For Starters
(10 minutes)

Discuss one of the following questions or give people a chance to say what struck them during the daily readings:

- "You never get a second chance to make a first impression," the saying goes. What might the first five to ten minutes of your worship services communicate to a stranger about who God is and why the community has gathered?

- What are some barriers that you face as you seek to bring your whole self into full participation in worship?

- In Isaiah 6:1-7, the prophet sees God and is filled with awe. Can you remember a time in worship when you felt awe? Share it with the members of your group.

Let's Focus
(5 minutes)

Read the introduction to this session; then have someone read the following focus statement aloud:

Isaiah 6 is the record of Isaiah's encounter with God. The prophet is brought into God's holy presence; he confesses sin, receives forgiveness, and later hears God's Word guiding him as he is sent back into the world. Today we study the first part of Isaiah's vision as a model for how we, as a congregation, can be made ready to hear God's Word and respond to it.

This encounter has three distinct components:

- When Isaiah encounters God, he enters a heavenly realm where worship is already taking place; he is overwhelmed by the sense of God's *holiness.*

- His immediate response is to become keenly aware of his own *unworthiness* to be in God's presence.

- God initiates an act of gracious forgiveness that enables Isaiah to receive God's Word and live.

Word Search

(20 minutes)

Many have seen the account in Isaiah 6 of the prophet's vision of God as a model for the Gathering stage of the church's worship. **Read aloud the following Scripture passages and briefly discuss the questions under each one (or formulate better ones of your own).**

- Isaiah 6:1-4
  Who initiates the visionary encounter between Isaiah and God? What's important about that?

  The angels are already worshiping as Isaiah enters the vision. What do you notice about the attitude and action of the angels?

  How might your congregational worship be participating in the worship of the whole earth and heaven?

  How do we or how could we increase this sense of participating in a much bigger worship in our church? Would it change how you feel about worship, or how important regular attendance is?

  In what ways do you perceive the ongoing worship of all creation?

How might we recognize in our worship services that we are joining something ongoing that is bigger than ourselves? Does this recognition change how we view the importance of our regular attendance at worship?

> **Word Alert**
>
> **Seraph** is a Hebrew word that identifies a particular sort of angel. The word has its roots in the word for fire, so one might call seraphs "burning ones." What might this tell you about the nature of God?

- Isaiah 6:5

Isaiah's natural response to God's overwhelming glory and holiness is *awe*. Awe is a combination of both attraction and fear. In his awe of God, Isaiah recognizes his own utter *lack* of holiness and he also recognizes that his *people* are unholy.

When do you most feel a fascination for and attraction to God's glory and holiness? Do other things in the world elicit in you a similar combination of fear and attraction? How and why?

When do you most feel a sense of fear and unworthiness? Do you ever feel a sense that you represent a *people* who are unholy? When?

- Isaiah 6:6-7

Forgiveness requires a painful process of cleansing. This process comes from God and prepares us to encounter God more fully.

What might the image of the coal on the lips suggest about the process of repentance and forgiveness?

How do you relate this to the basic Christian pattern of dying and rising?

What might this image suggest about worship?

Bring It Home

(15 minutes, or as time allows)

Choose one of the following options:

Option 1

You're a worship committee planning a service with the theme text Isaiah 6:1-7. You're responsible for the opening section ("Gathering"). **Plan what elements, hymns, songs, gestures, prayers, and so on you might use to help people experience God's call and enter into God's presence.**

Option 2

As time permits, **discuss the following questions in your group,** or formulate your own.

- Do you think of God primarily as One to be feared or as One who is our friend?

- Which of these does your congregation's worship emphasize? Are the two mutually exclusive?

Option 3

Draw a picture in which you imagine the live coal coming to touch either you or your congregation. Or perhaps replace the coal with another image that seems to fit your own congregation. What does it mean to be touched with this coal?

Pray It Through

(10 minutes)

Structure your prayer in three parts as follows. Perhaps three different people could pray, and all can observe a moment of silence between parts.

- Part 1: Join all creation in expressing adoration for God's holiness.

- Part 2: Acknowledge our own unworthiness before God.

- Part 3: Pray that we might be purified and that we might have courage to endure the Spirit's ways of preparing us to bear the glory of God's holy presence.

Live It Out
(10 minutes)

Write out the song of the angels from Isaiah 6:3, or from the doxology ("Praise God, from Whom All Blessings Flow"), or from the classic hymn "Holy! Holy! Holy! Lord God Almighty!" and place it where you can see it every day or carry it around with you. Let it remind you that you are always among the "creatures here below" and the "heavenly hosts above" who praise God.

(Web Alert)

Be sure to check out the participants' section for this session on our website, www.GrowDisciples.org, for interesting links and suggestions for readings and activities that will deepen your understanding of worship.

Session 3
Word

Monkey Minds

"Whoever has ears, let them hear."

—Matthew 13:9

Every once in a while I see an advertisement that uses a funny made-up word—televiserphonernetting—to describe (and poke gentle fun of) our modern tendency to multitask. A typical teenager today can take in a dozen visual images per second: watching TV out of the corner of her eye while writing an English paper at the computer, listening to music, and casually instant messaging—all at the same time. I know this is possible because my daughter does this.

Now, regardless of whether or not this sort of multitasking may be helpful for writing good English papers, it is without doubt an important skill for navigating our complex world. To keep up with a world that seems to fly by, it is crucial to be able to move quickly from one matter to another, to process input from multiple sources, to juggle numerous schedules.

As a result of all this fast-paced activity, it turns out that one of the hardest things to do is to slow down and give our full attention to *one thing*. My pastor says we have "monkey minds"—constantly jumping from branch to branch, tasting this, itching that, chattering and fidgeting.

Yet when the Scriptures are read and the sermon is preached, we need to focus and listen. The Reformers believed that everyone was capable of hearing and understanding the Word of God—people didn't need special education or skills to do so. At the same time, they also believed that we do need something special in order to really encounter Jesus in Scripture. We need the Holy Spirit.

During the Reformation, John Calvin introduced an important innovation into the church's worship: the prayer for illumination. This prayer asks the Holy Spirit to still our "monkey minds," to sweep away all those things than can prevent us from hearing, to illumine our darkness with the light of Christ.

In worship, "hearing" means much more than just registering the meaning of the words. To hear the Word of God is to invite it into our souls, to let it change us, to receive the comfort or judgment or guidance we need in that moment.

This kind of hearing requires grace. Even on our best days, we come to worship with gaps and dark spots in our faith, with anger and prideful resistance, with all sorts of private distractions. Without the Spirit's help, the Word is likely to fall on our rather rocky and weedy soil (see Matt. 13:1-9).

So we pray. We pray before the Scripture is read so that we might hear what God wishes to tell us through these words. We pray that our hearts may be soft, our minds sharp, our wills pliable.

We pray for both the reading of Scripture and for its proclamation in the sermon because both the preacher and the listener need God's help.

Anyone, not just the pastor, can offer the prayer for illumination, or the congregation could sing the prayer: "Open our eyes, Lord; we want to see Jesus."

The mystery of the incarnation is that the Word comes to us wherever and whenever and whoever we are. We pray before we listen to the Word of the Lord in order to prepare ourselves to receive that mystery.

Think It Over

1. Are you good at paying attention? In what circumstances are you able to give your full and undivided attention to something?

2. What sorts of things help or get in the way of your hearing the Scripture and sermon, in the fullest sense of hearing?

In Other Words

"[God] illumines our minds by the light of his Holy Spirit and opens our hearts for the Word and sacraments to enter in, which would otherwise only strike our ears and appear before our eyes, but not at all affect us within."

—John Calvin, *Institutes of the Christian Religion*, IV.3.10

Live It Out

Take time today to calm your own "monkey mind." Find a quiet corner or take a walk somewhere where you can be alone. Sit with your back straight, your hands still, and breathe slowly. Pray a prayer for illumination and then listen for God's Word to you. It may come from your own heart—memorized verses that God has hidden there. Or bring along a Bible and read a short passage from it, and then sit still again—for at least five completely silent minutes—focusing on hearing what God wants to say to you in that passage.

"Inky-plinky" (Worship Is Reverent) 2

"As the heavens are higher than the earth, so are my ways higher than your ways and my thoughts than your thoughts."

—Isaiah 55: 9

I once had the opportunity to introduce a group of college students to Matt Redman, a popular British worship leader and songwriter. Our group had a great discussion with Matt, during which he spoke candidly about some ways in which he was rethinking how he and his fellow contemporary artists composed worship songs. He recognized, for instance, the particular challenges of conveying awe with the guitar. "Love it or hate it," he said, "the organ tells us that it's a big God we worship. I can do intimacy on my guitar, but I can't do majesty. It just comes out 'inky-plinky.'"

Like every generation before us, we face the challenge of making our worship incarnational. If Jesus meets us in the here and now, then we desire to worship him in spoken and musical languages that we know. Many congregations have adopted the use of guitars, drums, and folk music idioms in worship for this very reason—because that is the musical language many people understand. As Matt observes, contemporary idioms of all kinds, like pop songs, black-box sanctuaries, and pastoral chatter, convey intimacy very well. And intimacy is surely part of our relationship with God—Jesus said, "I call you my friends."

Word Alert

Black-box sanctuaries refers to an industrial style of interior architecture in which the ductwork and other structural elements are exposed. Everything is painted black and there are no windows, so all the lighting is controlled, as in a theater.

But conveying God's majesty, grandeur, and mystery in worship is important too. As we saw in our study of Isaiah 6, an animating sense of respect and even fear is an appropriate and fitting response to an encounter with the holy. In Scripture, when people meet God they are usually deathly afraid. They hide their faces. They take off their shoes. They prepare to run in the other direction. Even angels who bring a message from God usually have to say "Fear not!" before anything else—because the person they're visiting is too busy being afraid to listen.

Perhaps it's more difficult in our day and age to convey a sense of God's grandeur than in ages past. Some older worship practices and places are especially good at conveying reverence for God: consider the otherworldly smell of incense, the magnificence of a cathedral space, the majesty of a full organ, the austerity and respect of prayer language that says to God, "How Great Thou Art." These things can remind us that God's ways are not our ways, that God is holy and not at all like us. They remind us, as some theologians put it, that God is wholly *other*.

But cultivating a reverent attitude to God's holy otherness in worship hardly requires an organ. You might listen to a slow, reverent reading of Scripture or participate in a vivid, concentrated dose of silence. Or kneel when you pray. Or take off your shoes upon entering the sanctuary. Or contemplate a large mural depicting Christ's return in glory. Or sing a song with words that remind us that when we worship we join "cherubim and seraphim, bowing down before him."

Our worship should remind us both of the nearness of God and of the power and distance of our holy, mysterious, transcendent God. Even when playful, it should acknowledge that the God we praise is an awesome God. If we neglect this, we too easily begin to worship a God who is too small, too "tame," too much in our image—instead of the other way around.

Think It Over

1. Recall an occasion in which you had a strong sense of the grandeur and majesty of God. What were your feelings at this time? Gratitude? Wonder? Adoration?

2. Have you ever felt a strong sense of fear of God?

In Other Words

"On the whole, I do not find Christians, outside of the catacombs, sufficiently sensible of conditions. Does anyone have the foggiest idea what sort of power we so blithely invoke? Or, as I suspect, does no one believe a word of it? The churches are children playing on the floor with their chemistry sets, mixing up a batch of TNT to kill a Sunday morning. It is madness to wear ladies' straw hats and velvet hats to church; we should all be wearing crash helmets."

—Annie Dillard, *Teaching a Stone to Talk*

Live It Out

In Scripture, people are often described as falling face down on the ground when encountering God. Today, pray for at least five minutes while you lie face down on the ground, arms spread wide. Does assuming this posture change how you experience God as you pray?

Ink into Blood 3

*"My soul faints with longing for your salvation,
but I have put my hope in your word."*
—Psalm 119:81

When I attended a bar mitzvah a few years ago, I got to experience a wonderful way these "people of the Book" express their longing for and love of God's word: before the Torah is read, it is removed from its prominent place in the front of the synagogue. Then, as joyful music plays, the scroll is paraded among the congregation, up and down the aisles, where people stand up from their seats to see it, to reach out to touch it, and even to kiss it.

> **Word Alert**
> The *Torah* is the first five books of the Old Testament: Genesis, Exodus, Leviticus, Numbers, Deuteronomy; it's also called the Book of Moses or the Law of Moses.

We Christians inherited a love of the Scriptures from our Jewish brothers and sisters. We too give a central place in our worship to reading from this strange, wonderful, holy book.

And let's be honest: the Bible *is* strange. Written in ancient foreign languages, it is filled with a beautifully odd mix of Hebrew poetry and colorful history, prophecy and prayer and parables, mystic visions, ethical instructions, and beloved stories. We struggle to wrap our tongues around names like Zerubbabel and to wrap our minds around Paul's sometimes convoluted grammar. We struggle to wrap our hearts around difficult instructions like "love your enemies."

Yet in its very strangeness, the Bible pulls us out of our self-centeredness and puts us in the middle of something much bigger than us. Each time we hear a passage of Scripture, we are learning God's perspective on the world, looking through a window on the whole sweep of redemption history. We are hearing and seeing *God's* story and finding our place in it.

And that's what makes it not just strange, but holy. We read from Scripture in worship because it is both the record of revelation to God's people in the past—and because it is God's active, living revelation to us *now*. That's why good preachers base their sermons not on the latest book they're reading but on *this* lasting book.

In Scripture, whether read in worship by the pastor, spoken by the congregation, or sung by the choir, it is *God* who speaks—to bless, to caution, to encourage or teach or comfort or challenge. Sometimes a phrase will jump out as if the Holy Spirit means to whisper it directly into our hearts. The reading of Scripture becomes, by God's grace, a *hearing* of the divine Word.

No wonder we put the reading of Scripture at the center of Christian worship! In fact, there are some Christian traditions whose love of Scripture is expressed in a way that borrows heavily from the Jewish traditions described earlier. At the beginning of worship, a large and beautifully bound Bible is processed up the aisle to the front of the sanctuary. When the time comes to read from the Gospels, the reader holds the book aloft and brings it from the front into the midst of the congregation, where everyone stands attentively as it is read aloud. Other traditions insist that Scripture always be *sung*—simply and beautifully—to acknowledge that this is God's Word; it is elevated language, distinguished from normal speech.

I'm always grateful for those congregations whose worship practices strive to help us savor Scripture. Some congregations use pastors or others in the congregation who are gifted at public speaking to read Scripture slowly and expressively, as if it were precious honey to be dripped into the waiting mouths of the people. Some congregations read Scripture responsively verse by verse, emphasizing that it belongs to all God's people. Some read from noble and dignified translations, some from plain-text paraphrases. There are good reasons for all of these things, but in the end, the words of the Bible are just ink on the page. We honor those black marks, but that's not what we worship.

The printed words we read are only the trace of where the Spirit has been and where the Spirit will be again, over and over, according to God's promise. The words become the Word of God for us when breathed with human breath and through the Spirit's power—when we read them together, when we take them into ourselves, body and soul. Then God can transform those words into our life-blood: our hearts, our actions, our whole way of being.

Think It Over

1. When you encounter Scripture, is it something you seek to understand or explain? Or do you think of it more as a gift to be received?

2. How can you experience God's Word spoken directly *to you* in your life situation?

3. How might you listen for God's Word as a way to get a God's-eye view of the world?

In Other Words

"Approach the Scriptures not so much as a manual of Christian principles but as the testimony of God's friends on what it means to walk with him through a thousand different episodes. When you are at war, when you are in love, when you have sinned, when you have been given a great gift—this is how you walk with God."

—John Eldridge, *Waking the Dead*

Live It Out

Create a prominent space at home for your Bible—perhaps on a small stand with a candle or greens or other seasonal decorations. Then, when you read the Bible in your home, either individually or as a family, create a spirit of joyful reverence and expectation by taking the Bible down to read it—maybe you could light the candle, or sing a song, or begin with a few seconds of silence.

Sails Raised and Trimmed (Worship Is Expectant) 4

"Yet a time is coming and has now come when the true worshipers will worship the Father in the Spirit and in truth, for they are the kind of worshipers the Father seeks. God is spirit, and his worshipers must worship in the Spirit and in truth."

—John 4:23-24

The Christian satire website Lark News once ran an "article" about a congregation that had finally managed to make everyone completely happy with the church's music program: they had installed an animatronic worship band. That's right, a

> **Word Alert**
>
> *Animatronics* is the term for a form of robotics first created by Walt Disney Imagineering for shows and attractions at theme parks. The robots move and make noise, generally in speech or song.

worship band made of robots, like the "Country Bear Jamboree" at Disney. Their music was always flawless, they played only what the congregation programmed them to play, and they never ever quarreled with anyone. Everyone knew exactly what to expect, and everyone's expectations were perfectly met.

We all have expectations when we come to worship. Maybe we expect beautiful choral anthems, or a solid dose of biblical teaching, or a warm feeling of belonging among people we know.

And we've all had days when those expectations were disappointed. That's because the people leading and attending worship aren't programmable. Preachers have off days, musicians hit wrong notes, kids squirm in their seats, and grown-ups are full of distractions. When you think about it, it's a wonder anything divine ever happens in worship.

It *is* a wonder! It's a wonder of the Spirit's work. The Spirit blows where it will, as Jesus said. We can't make it happen. We don't engineer the Spirit's presence—not with scholarly exegesis or pitch-perfect choirs, not with candle-lit ambiance or homemade bread or a stack of amplifiers.

But we can *expect* it.

How do we do that? Certainly we can offer to God our best work as worship planners and leaders and our most excellent efforts and earnest presence as worshipers. But mostly we can simply cultivate an attitude of humble expectation. We can come to worship with our sails raised and trimmed, awaiting the wind of the Spirit. Then when it comes—as a gale or as a gentle breeze—we're prepared to catch as much of it as we're able.

There's no denying that some worship services seem more "eventful" than others. Maybe that eventfulness is experienced as sharper insight into the gospel, or deeper love for Jesus, or keener motivation to feed the hungry and care for the poor.

We don't always know why this is so. Too many factors come into play to puzzle it out. This should not be discouraging to us; it reminds us that we are human and that God is sovereign. If we could always push the right buttons to "bring God in the house" or to bring the congregation "to the next level," our worship would be a bit too animatronic.

The Spirit blows where it will, so we worship with our sails raised and trimmed, expecting great things of God, and enjoying, rather than engineering, a contagious spiritual energy.

Certainly we should have expectations for worship—not so much for the behavior of those leading worship or even of ourselves, but expectations that God will work, sometimes through our very best efforts and sometimes despite our worst, because they are joined to the perfect worship of Christ. In the end, it's not about our hard work, but God's.

The Father seeks out worshipers "in the Spirit and in truth" (John 4:24). We can gather to worship trusting in the sovereign grace of God. We can work hard at the liturgy (the "work of the people") as though it depended on us but realizing, thankfully, that it does not. And in the end, we can humbly allow ourselves to be blown by the steady wind or unpredictable gusts of the Spirit.

Think It Over

1. What do you expect when you go to worship?

2. What are the elements that contribute to a "good" worship experience for you? What happens in the service? What happens in you?

3. When you have a disappointing experience in worship, to what do you usually attribute that?

In Other Words

"We're not *going to church*; YOU *are* the Church—and we go to worship so that we learn how to be Church."

—Marva Dawn, *A Royal "Waste" of Time*

Live It Out

Take some time each day to think about the coming worship service. If you know the Scripture or theme (if not, call the church and find out), read it and reflect on it. Pray each day for God to open your heart and mind for true worship that Sunday.

The Juggling Jesus 5

"We preach Christ crucified: a stumbling block to Jews and foolishness to Gentiles, but to those whom God has called, both Jews and Greeks, Christ the power of God and the wisdom of God."
—1 Corinthians 1:23-24

"Faith comes from hearing the message, and the message is heard through the word about Christ."
—Romans 10:17

Worshiping a few years ago at church, I looked over to see my son drawing on the children's bulletin during the sermon. The cover of the bulletin depicted Jesus in a boat on the Sea of Galilee, preaching to the crowds. Philip had drawn some dark blobs near Jesus' hands. "What are those, Pip?" I whispered. "Those are rubber balls," he said. "Jesus is juggling."

Hmmm, I thought. If *Jesus* has to juggle to keep the congregation's attention, the church is in big trouble.

I know the "juggling Jesus" problem from both sides of the pulpit. As a preacher competing with NFL Sunday and YouTube (not to mention the church down the street), I am familiar with the temptation to entertain the crowd instead of to proclaim the gospel, to try get folks to say "Wow" instead of "Hallelujah!" And as a worshiper in the pew, I have sat quietly fuming while the preacher waves his arms and scolds the congregation, or talks about "six

Word Alert

YouTube **is a video sharing website created in February 2005 where users can upload, view, and share video clips.**

steps to find your soul mate," but has very little to say about the Bible and of the life of following Jesus.

Of course, there's nothing wrong with a sermon that is practical or doctrinal or even entertaining. In one of the very first sermon instruction manuals, Saint Augustine wrote that a sermon should do what any good speech does: delight, teach, and inspire. But it does these things on the way toward the central thing the sermon does: that is, to speak God's good news in Christ for us. That's more than just good advice for preachers; it's also a roadmap for listeners.

When listening to a sermon, see if you can hear first of all the proclamation of the *gospel*—that is, good news. It may begin as bad news: the world is a desperate and dangerous place, and we are sinful through and through. But listen for where the sermon declares God's promised presence, God's steadfast love, God's amazing grace. Listen for where the sermon invites and prompts faith in those who have not heard the story before. And listen for your own heart, thrumming in sympathetic vibration when you hear the good news sung by the preacher.

Listen, though, not just for *any* good news. A sermon is the good news *in Christ.* The apostle Paul said that his preaching was centered on Christ crucified, the power of God, and the wisdom of God. So the best preachers always start with Scripture, end with Scripture, and in the middle stay very close to Scripture, the story of God's saving love as it culminates in Jesus' life and death and resurrection.

When you hear a sermon that isn't rooted in the Bible, it might be a good talk with some Christian content, but it's not preaching. On the other hand, when we hear the pastor opening up Scripture—explaining it, exploring it, and applying it—we experience the living Word of God. This doesn't mean that we agree with everything the pastor says, or that the words of the sermon have the same authority as Jesus' words. But we ought to expect the preacher to preach from the Bible. And in every sermon we should expect to hear a word from God for us.

Because in the end, a sermon is the good news in Christ *for us*. It isn't a speech about abstract principles of justice and peace and joy. A sermon meets us exactly where we are, in all the details of our lives: concerned about our finances, afraid of getting old, excited about the start of a new school year, grieving lost friends or lost hopes. In the sermon Jesus comes to us, as he once came to the disciples on the way to Emmaus, to show us what God's Word has to do with our lives, to illumine the road we're on. It consoles us, warns us, teaches us, stirs us to action, and equips us to fulfill our callings. It speaks a *living* Word.

The Holy Spirit makes all that happen. It's not the preacher and it's not the congregation, though they both have their roles. Yes, the Word of God comes in the words of the preacher and is encouraged and embraced by an expectant congregation. But the heavy lifting isn't up to us. The Word comes alive in our hearts somewhere *between* the preacher's lips and the congregation's ears, in the whisper of the Holy Spirit, speaking the good news of Christ for us.

Think It Over

1. Think about some of the kinds of sermons you've listened to. Try to list a variety, and put them in a line from worst to best. What were the ingredients that made for the best sermons? (But don't get down on the preacher—they all have their "off" days!)

2. Would you say you have had encounters with the living Christ through listening to preaching? Describe.

In Other Words

"A congregation can make or break a sermon by the quality of their response to it. An inspired sermon can wind up skewered somewhere near the second pew by a congregation of people who sit with their arms crossed and their eyes narrowed, coughing and scuffing their feet as the preacher struggles to be heard. Similarly, a weak sermon can grow strong in the presence of people who attend carefully to it, leaning forward in their pews and opening their faces to a preacher from whom they clearly expect to hear good news."

—Barbara Brown Taylor, *The Preaching Life*

Live It Out

Write your preacher a note of encouragement and thanks today.

Session 3
Active Listening
Discussion Guide

In many African-American congregations, according to Evans Crawford, when a preacher is having difficulty articulating the gospel, the congregation doesn't sit back and wince—they pray. Out loud. "Help him, Jesus!" they call out. As the preacher begins to hint at the good news, they call out encouragement: "Well? That's all right!" And when the Holy Spirit begins to speak boldly and clearly, they shout their praise to God: "Amen! Glory, Hallelujah!"

These congregations know, perhaps better than many other Christian traditions, that preaching is a cooperative enterprise between the preacher and an active congregation and an even more active Holy Spirit. Last week we considered what it means to gather as a people before God. This week, we move to the next stage of the worship service, the active, cooperative work of proclamation.

We've already explored the importance of praying for the Spirit's help in hearing the Word. We discussed the importance of reverence in worship, an attitude of awe before God. We thought about the expectations we bring to worship and refocused them on God's action. Finally, we pondered the mystery of the Word as it comes to us through the reading of Scripture and through preaching.

Nehemiah 8-9 describes an important transition point for the people of Israel. Having experienced a long, painful exile in Babylon, they are finally returning to their land and trying to reestablish a settled worship life. The story of Ezra reading the Book of Moses to the people reminds us of several important characteristics of the proclamation of the Word that we can apply to our own worship services.

For Starters
(10 minutes)

Discuss one of the following questions, or something else sparked by the daily devotions:

1. The book of Hebrews declares that "the word of God is alive and active. Sharper than any two-edged sword, it penetrates even to dividing soul and spirit, joints and marrow; it judges the thoughts and attitudes of the heart" (4:12). Have you ever felt the Word of God like a sword in your heart? What are some other metaphors to describe how the Word of God has spoken to you?

Let's Focus
(5 minutes)

Read the introduction to this session, and then have someone read this focus statement aloud:

The picture in Nehemiah 8 of a tired and thirsty people shows us at least four elements in the process of proclaiming the Word. First, the people feel their need for the Word. Then they hear and respond—very actively. Next, the word is interpreted for them. Finally, they respond with joy.

Word Search
(20 minutes)

Many have seen Nehemiah 8-9, an account of Ezra reading the law to the returned exiles, as a model for the church's encounter with God in the Word. **Read aloud the following Scripture passages and briefly discuss the questions under each one (or formulate better ones of your own).**

- Nehemiah 8:1-3
  Previously the returned exiles had been busy at work in different locations on the city walls, but now they were "settled in their own towns" (7:73). They came together in the square before the Water Gate and asked Ezra to read the holy book.

  Why do you think the writer mentions several times that *all* the people assembled (not just the men, which was more typically the custom)?

  What does their attentive listening suggest about what they expect from the reading?

- Nehemiah 8:4-6
  Ezra reads the record of God's acts and promises, as well as God's requirements for holy living. It is likely the people had rarely had opportunity to hear this book read while in captivity.

  What does the people's response to the reading suggest about their emotions on this occasion?

  What kinds of things does your congregation do in worship that are similar to this response?

- Nehemiah 8:7-8
  The Levites helped Ezra by interpreting the Book of the Law for the people. In our worship practices, this process of interpretation has its equivalent in preaching.

  Why was interpretation necessary for these returned exiles?

  Why is preaching necessary for us?

- Nehemiah 8:9-12
  It seems the people first wanted to respond with sorrow over the reading of the book. Why do you suppose that would be?

  Nehemiah insists that the people rejoice instead. Why? In what way does your congregation express joy in the hearing of the Word?

Bring It Home

(15 minutes, or as time allows)

Choose one of the following options:

Option 1

Discuss practical ways that your congregation could help one another prepare for worship each week and help one another "listen attentively" for the Word during the service. For example, the week before, you might read the Scripture passage upon which the sermon will be based and let it sink into your heart each day for ten minutes. What else might you do?

Option 2

Invite the whole group to act as a sermon planning committee. Read Mark 4: 35-41 and have Bibles for everyone to refer to. Have someone write the group's suggestions on a board or on newsprint.

- How would you engage the interest of the congregation in this text?

- What's the warning here, and how would you apply it?

- What's the "gospel" here, and how would you express it?

- What could you say to get in touch with where many in the congregation might be spiritually or emotionally?

Option 3

Take some of the metaphors mentioned in the group during the initial discussion (what is the Word of God like?) and act them out. Or draw a series of pictures to depict the many ways that the Word speaks to us.

Pray It Through

(10 minutes)

Divide these prayer ideas among the group, or pray each one and allow a time of silence between them so that each person can silently affirm what is said.

• Pray that your congregation will come to worship with a spirit of expectation to hear the Word.

• Pray for those who read Scripture and preach.

• Pray for the Spirit's guidance in interpreting what the Word means for your congregation today.

• Pray that you might be led to respond joyfully to the Word.

Live It Out

(10 minutes)

If your group chose option 1 above, select one of the ideas you talked about to help each other listen attentively to the Word—and do it. Tell someone else in your group what you will do, and hold each other accountable.

If you didn't select option 1 above, decide what you will do to help sharpen your expectant listening next Sunday, or think about it and decide for yourself.

> (Web Alert)
>
> **Be sure to check out the participants' section for this session on our website, www.GrowDisciples.org, for interesting links and suggestions for readings and activities that will deepen your understanding of worship.**

Session 4
Response

Paper, People, Priest, Prayer 1

"Do not be anxious about anything, but in every situation, by prayer and petition, with thanksgiving, present your requests to God."

—Philippians 4:6

The small sanctuary is dimly lit. In the middle of the worship space a white sheet is draped over a table. A large, homemade Christ candle sits at the very center, and a repeating image of Christ at prayer is projected from above. As quiet music plays, members of the congregation page through sections of the day's newspaper. Periodically, someone tears out a story—maybe about the local teachers' strike, or a person arrested for drunk driving—holds it for a moment, and then comes forward to lay it carefully on the sheet. After about ten minutes, the congregation holds out their hands over the impromptu artwork, and they sing together: "O Lord, hear our prayer."

I experienced this unusual but beautiful intercessory prayer a few years ago when I was visiting a church in England known for its creative worship practices. Most congregations have a significant moment in the weekly worship service when the church comes to God with its own needs and the needs of the world. Most, however, employ a designated "pray-er" and articulate their concerns with spoken words. What I experienced that day was different from what most of us are used to. Still, it can teach us some important truths about the way the church, "by prayer and petition," presents its requests to God.

First, there was no clear "leader." This seems exactly right, because the intercessory prayer belongs to *all* God's people. Other names used for this prayer suggest this too: *congregational prayer, prayers of the people,* or *pastoral prayer* (not the *pastor's prayer*). Even when spoken by a single voice, it is the responsibility and privilege of the entire congregation to join their prayers with the constant, universal prayer of the communion of saints. Some congregations express the communal character of the prayer by having the leader pray not from the front of the sanctuary, but from the middle of the congregation, or by asking the congregation to affirm the prayers spoken by the leader by singing or saying "Amen" or "Lord, hear our prayer."

Second, the backdrop for our prayer that day was a Christ candle and Christ's projected image. This reminds us that the church has a *priestly* role in the world; part of our job is to bring the needs of the world before God, to "re-present" them, interceding in something of the same way that the high priests of ancient Israel interceded for the people, asking for justice and mercy. Jesus is the true high priest, we know. But as the body of Christ, we imitate Christ in his priestly ministry. Some congregations underscore this theological truth by structuring this prayer after the Lord's Prayer, or by remembering carefully in prayer those who were the special concern of Jesus: the poor and the outcast, the helpless and the hopeless.

Third, the needs brought to God in prayer that day arose both from our immediate horizon and horizons beyond. When we pray together we bring to God the anxieties that arise from our own situations, and we bring prayers for wholeness for those whom we know. We also seek God's blessing on our church's ministries. But more than this—we pray to expand our horizons, to represent the whole broken world. We pray for our communities and our nation, for people both near and far, for those who can't pray and those who won't, for both friend—and, as Jesus taught, foe. Praying in this way

> **Word Alert**
>
> **In the Reformed tradition we do not have priests, so we're not so familiar with the *priestly* role. In the Old Testament the priest, especially the High Priest, served as an intermediary between God and the people. For example, he brought the sacrifices of the people and spoke God's blessing to them. Christ is the perfect High Priest, and the Bible says we are now "priests to serve his God and Father" (Rev. 1:6).**

helps deepen our sense of a divine love that embraces wider than our arms can reach.

Finally, we pray in hope, even when we can't fully articulate what that hope is. Those of us praying the newspaper prayer laid next to the Christ candle stories about overcrowded prisons, for example. But what was the content of our prayers? That those in prison may know the freedom of Christ? That the jailers treat them with fairness? That our society pursue restorative rather than retributive justice? All of these, perhaps, and more, as in our silence, the Holy Spirit prayed in sighs deeper than our words.

Think It Over

Perhaps you've seen one of these amazing satellite photographs of the earth from space taken at night. The lights are highly concentrated in the most populated areas of the earth. Imagine what the earth might look like from space if lights would shine wherever churches were praying together. What might that look like?

In Other Words

"When you pray, you are not starting the conversation from scratch, just remembering to plug back into a conversation that's always in progress."

—Anne Lamott, *Plan B, Further Thoughts on Faith*

Live It Out

Pray today with the newspaper. Tear out headlines that represent what you wish to bring to God. Set up a place to lay them, perhaps with a candle, and let your action and quiet thought be your prayer.

Singing with the Humpback Whale (Worship Is Expansive) 2

"After this I looked, and there before me was a great multitude that no one could count, from every nation, tribe, people and language, standing before the throne and in front of the Lamb."

—Revelation 7:9

One of my favorite churches is the beautiful Cathedral of Our Lady of the Angels in Los Angeles, California. I especially love the majestic, earth-toned tapestries hung along each side of the nave. The tapestries depict 135 saints and holy people representing every age and region of the world. They are hung so that the figures all stand facing the front of the cathedral with hands raised in prayer. There are ancient saints such as Augustine and recognizable modern saints such as Mother Teresa. The artist used men, women, and children of all races as models, giving his figures a realism that celebrates the diversity and beauty of all people. The artwork is called "The Communion of the Saints."

What a vivid reminder that whenever we worship, we are joining the ceaseless worship of God in all times and places!

Word Alert

In traditional Gothic church architecture, the *nave* is the long central part of the building that forms the main interior space up to the altar or chancel. If you imagine the floor plan as a cross shape, it's the longest part of the cross.

When you and I worship, we join Christians in Sierra Leone and Prince Edward Island, in Sri Lanka and Romania and Venezuela. We join Syrian Christians from the second century and French Christians from the twelfth century. We join all the heavenly hosts and creatures on earth below to give our doxology, our praise to our God. No matter how small and plain and ordinary our particular congregation, we are still part of this glorious throng.

And there's more. Scripture declares that all creation offers to God its song of praise and its cry of lament. The heavens declare God's glory and the stars sing praise; the mountains shout for joy and the beasts in the sea groan with eager longing for final redemption. The worship we offer isn't just local or global— it's *cosmic*.

This puts into perspective, doesn't it, the desire we sometimes indulge for worship to serve our own needs? To satisfy our personal tastes for a certain kind of music or preaching or visual style? Of course worship should be expressive and comfortable for us—to a point. But especially in our "have it your way" culture, it's good to be reminded that worship is *not about us*.

In our worship we dip our toes in an endless stream of worship that flows from all times and places toward God. Our worship, then, should be expansive. It should participate in and point to the coming kingdom of God, where people from every tribe and nation and people and tongue shall gather round the throne in praise, bringing their gifts.

We demonstrate and cultivate this expansiveness through song, prayer, language, art, and in many other ways. We make creative and excellent use of words and music and more from many times, places, peoples, and cultures to enlarge our vision of God's kingdom and to situate ourselves properly and humbly within it.

For example, when I am in charge of worship planning, I always select some music the congregation knows well—using the musical language that comes easiest to them. But I am also careful to reach out in time and place to include hymns and prayer texts from the past, from saints who ran the race before us, as well as from our brothers and sisters in other places: a prayer of protest from South Africa, a song of adoration from Argentina, a song of faithfulness from Japan. When we sing in their accents, we prepare ourselves for our final destiny when we join them singing a universal song of wonder, love, and praise.

Think It Over

If you were to create tapestries for your own church's sanctuary depicting saints from all times and places, who would you depict? Your parents or grandparents? Figures from the Bible? A Christian from history whom you admire?

In Other Words

"The family of God trots the globe and spans the centuries. . . . Our union with Christ joins us not just to those who were baptized last Sunday morning, nor with those to whom we passed the cup and loaf. We are also one with Adam and Eve, and Abraham and Sarah, and David, Isaiah, and Ruth. We are one with . . . Parthians, Medes, and Elamites who were cut to the heart after hearing Peter's Pentcost [sermon] one windy day in Jerusalem. We are one with martyrs, the reformers, and the revivalists. One with believers on every continent, yesterday, today, and tomorrow."

—Cornelius Plantinga Jr. and Sue A. Roozeboom, *Discerning the Spirits*

Live It Out

Think of a time in history or another part of the world that is especially important to you—perhaps your family's place of origin. Find or create an object to remind you of that time or place and have it near you when you pray today: a photograph, a book, a pair of old glasses, a rock, an item of clothing. If possible, bring the object with you to church this week and let it remind you that your worship joins in the worldwide worship of God.

Count the Cost 3

"I will sacrifice a thank offering to you and call on the name of the LORD. I will fulfill my vows to the LORD in the presence of all his people."

—Psalm 116:17-18

I visited a church a couple years ago where they did the most extraordinary thing at the offering. Instead of passing the offering plates and then bringing them up front while singing the doxology, they passed the plates while two families came forward to bring testimony. The testimonies explained what the families had done with their share of an offering that had been taken some weeks before. Apparently as a response to a sermon on the parable of the talents, that week's offering had been divided up and given *back* to the various households of the church. They were then instructed to use their share to invest in the kingdom.

One family told of how they had decided to buy a sheep through the Heifer Project. But they didn't have enough money to do it. So each of the family members figured out a way to earn more. They did the typical things: the teenage son mowed lawns, the young daughter set up a lemonade stand. In the end, the family augmented what they had been given and had enough for the sheep and a few chickens too.

These testimonies beautifully demonstrated that the ritual of offering is meant to be a token of something much bigger. Yes, it's important that we give our money away to causes that advance the kingdom, including the upkeep of our church and the support of its ministries. But the offering represents the giving of our whole lives in response to God's grace given first to us.

That's why the offering (not "collection") most often comes toward the end of the service. It's not to thank the preacher for a good sermon or the praise team for a hot performance. Neither is it simply a matter of taking care of church business and making sure the bills get paid. Instead, the offering is our response to God's grace; it symbolizes the way we "offer ourselves as living sacrifices." The offering connects our adoration with discipleship.

I loved the way these families' testimonies revealed how getting the money back on that previous week had prompted them to do something beyond writing a check. They had to think and be creative and take some action.

Their stories also showed that God loves to multiply our efforts, just as Jesus multiplied the loaves and fishes. The offering money expanded—it got bigger, but it also expanded far beyond the congregation. A family somewhere in Gambia received a valuable animal because of a church in California. This church illustrated beautifully that God loves to spread our small efforts outward like ripples on a pond.

Sometimes offering ourselves as living sacrifices is not easy. I particularly recall a line from a service in my Iona worship book: "I will not offer to God a sacrifice that costs me nothing." Whether placing hard-earned dollars in the offering plate is easy or uncomfortable for us, this act reminds us that offering ourselves sometimes feels joyful and sometimes feels like a sacrifice. It can hurt.

Word Alert

Iona is an ecumenical Christian community of men and women from different walks of life and different traditions in the Christian church committed to seeking new ways of living the gospel of Jesus in today's world. It's located on the island of Iona off the coast of Scotland, and it offers hospitality to the many pilgrims who come to worship there.

In my church, individuals or representatives of each family bring offerings forward just before we begin the part of the service where we celebrate communion. This signals that even as we are responding in thanks to God's Word, God is busy setting a table of grace for us. Our thankfulness is caught up into God's grace, broken and multiplied and offered to the world.

Think It Over

1. Is money the hardest thing for you to give up to God? If not, what is?

2. In what way are you offering to God a sacrifice that actually costs you something?

In Other Words

"Then we all rise together and pray, and, as we before said, when our prayer is ended, bread and wine and water are brought, and the president in like manner offers prayers and thanksgivings, according to his ability, and the people assent, saying Amen; and there is a distribution to each, and a participation of that over which thanks have been given, and to those who are absent a portion is sent by the deacons. And they who are well-to-do, and willing, give what each thinks fit; and what is collected is deposited with the president, who [gives assistance to] the orphans and widows, and those who, through sickness or any other cause are in want, and those who are in bonds, and the strangers sojourning among us, and in a word takes care of all who are in need."

—Justin Martyr (A.D. 110-165)

Live It Out

Get your offering ready for Sunday's service today. If it's time to reassess how you prioritize giving in your budget, take a step toward that today. Have a dinner-table discussion, check out a book from the library, get some good counsel from someone you trust.

Matter Matters (Worship Is Sacramental) 4

"Taste and see that the Lord is good."

—Psalm 34:8

I wonder how you would respond if your pastor opened the worship service this Sunday by making the following announcement: "Congregation in the Lord Jesus Christ, please remain seated. Today we are not going to sing any songs. Instead, when the time comes for a song, please refer to the words on the screen and simply think them. Sing the song in your hearts in silence."

This might seem like a silly idea—after all, many of us love singing in worship. But if someone were to suggest that thinking about the words—really thinking them *hard*—might be more spiritual than singing, would you be tempted to agree? Would you want to worship that way?

Since the Reformation, Protestants have had a strong tendency to value thoughts and beliefs (and secondarily, feelings) as more spiritual than . . . well, *things*. With more than a trace of anti-Catholicism in our DNA, we tend to see church architecture, art, music, and even our physical actions in worship as, at best, helpful aids or reminders to transcendent truths. At worst, they are distractions from the real business of being spiritual.

When we fall into this dualist trap, however, we are forgetting one of the central mysteries of Christianity: the Incarnation. God not only created the world, but God also cared enough about it to enter it. It was, in the words of preacher Frederick Buechner, a uniform he wasn't ashamed to wear. And still more remarkable: this matter will not be left behind when Jesus returns to make all things new. Christians believe in the resurrection of *the body*, not some super-spiritual soul freed from its limitations, but an imperishable body to live in an imperishable earth.

Word Alert

Dualists **divide the world too sharply into the material and the spiritual, the secular and the sacred in a way that obscures the fact that God made all things, "seen and unseen" (Nicene Creed). God also communicates with us through the physical as well as the spiritual.**

Matter mattered in the beginning; and because of Christ, matter matters more. The Word became flesh, so that in the flesh we might see God.

This has explosive implications. It means that *things* can be avenues of grace—not only mountain lakes and beautiful sunsets, but also a baby's tiny fists, or full-throated singing, or the smell of a lily, or a fountain of burbling water, or bread and wine. The Incarnation restores the potential transparency of things to the beauty and glory of God.

In worship, then, we can eagerly bring the skills and pleasures and needs of our physical selves, our *senses.* God-praising violins and dancing and a child's crayon drawing and our own growling stomachs are no less spiritual than our God-directed thoughts and feelings. The ordinary things of life can point us to the wonder of God's presence.

Condescending to our materiality, God engages us in worship through physical things—through art and music, through the spoken word, touch and taste, bread and water and wine.

We employ them as expressive tools; God redeems them as channels of grace.

Most of all, when we observe and celebrate the sacraments we realize the intimate connection between the spiritual and the material. But by getting into the habit of seeking grace in ordinary things, we are better able to experience the real presence of Christ in baptism and communion, where ordinary things—bread and wine and water—are attached to God's covenant promises. The sacraments then become more than simply symbols or reminders—devotional aids with no real transformative power. Instead, they will be opened as channels of God's saving grace for us, body and soul, in life and in death.

Think It Over

1. If you were instructed to spend an hour being as spiritual as possible, what would you do?

2. Does your plan try to avoid the physical dimension or does it embrace it?

In Other Words

"In the church where we go to now
people are so hungry and thirsty
they stand in line
for a bite of bread,
a single sip . . ."

—John Terpstra, "Desert," *Brendan Luck*

Live It Out

Practice seeing God's common grace in ordinary things today. Arrange some flowers in a vase, or pay special attention to the way your body works as you exercise.

Do This 5

"I am the living bread that came down from heaven. Whoever eats of this bread will live forever. This bread is my flesh, which I will give for the life of the world."

—John 6:51

I was teaching a course on worship, and our class was discussing the Lord's Supper. "What has been your experience of this sacrament?" I asked. Students connected the meal to moments of spiritual significance for them, moments when they grasped—deeply and intuitively—the unity of the church, or the promise of eternal life, or the love shown in Jesus' sacrifice. But one student admitted that she didn't like the Sundays when her church celebrated this sacrament. "The services last too long," she said.

I was speechless. After years of participating in communion every week at my home church, I have grown to treasure it. It feeds my soul in ways that nothing else can; it has changed me in ways beyond words. Her experience was just the opposite. On the rare occasions when her church does celebrate the sacrament, it feels to her like a waste of time. What Jesus meant for us as the deepest nourishment, she experienced as a nuisance.

I cannot explain why some people have this experience, but I wonder if it has something to do with what we expect, what we think does or does not happen during the meal. Is God really active at the meal, or are we just remembering what God did in the past? When we obey Jesus' command "Do this," the question is: does *God* do anything? The church has always said yes.

First, God hosts us at a covenant meal called "the Lord's Supper." This name for the sacrament emphasizes its origins in Jesus' Passover meal with his disciples. The accent is on God making available to us now what Jesus did in the sacrifice of his body and blood to rescue us from sin. And just as Christ was present when he gave the church this meal, Christ is present each time we celebrate it: by the power of the Holy Spirit, we are lifted spiritually into the presence of Christ, seated at God's right hand. God feeds our souls and gives us a glimpse of eternity.

Second, God unites us into the body of Christ. We also call this meal "Holy Communion," which emphasizes its relational element. When we eat and drink together, we have communion with one another and with Christ. Though we may indeed find it a personally moving experience, it is never private: "We, who are many, are one body, for we all partake of the one loaf" (1 Cor. 10:17). Through baptism, God brings us into a set-apart community; through communion the Holy Spirit sustains us in it.

Third, God gives and promises us grace. Another term used for the meal is "Eucharist." This term has roots in words that mean "good grace" and "thanksgiving." It connects the meal to the prayer of thanksgiving—the "grace"—that is often said before eating. Thus it suggests that even as we share the bread and wine God gave to us in the first place, God turns around and gives them back to us *again*, where we receive them as "the bread of heaven and the cup of salvation," a sign and seal of a new covenant and its promises of forgiveness and resurrection. All this points to the spirit of celebration and hope in which we enjoy the meal.

God does all these things through the varied ways we choose to enact this meal. In some congregations, for example, the bread and wine are divided into small portions and passed to the congregation sitting in the pew. In others the congregation comes forward and kneels while receiving the elements from the pastor and elders. In other places worshipers stand in a circle and pass the gifts to each other, saying "This is Christ's body and blood, given for you." Some use large loaves of Jewish Challah bread, others flat pressed wafers; some sip grape juice out of plastic cups, others pour wine into ceramic goblets. Some commune in silence, others surround themselves with music.

Some of these ways may more fully express certain meanings of the meal, and some may enable us to be more aware of God's promised presence. But ultimately this meal—whatever we call it and however we enact it—is a mystery. Like baptism, it gathers up our ordinary, fleshly lives into eternal realities in ways no amount of careful theology can fully explain.

The Lord's Supper is not a mere *reminder* but a *means* of God's grace. The most important thing is not to understand it correctly or celebrate it in exactly the right way. Instead, we should obey Jesus' command: Do this. When we practice it joyfully and well (and, I might suggest, frequently), we open ourselves more and more to the mystery of God's grace.

Think It Over

If for some reason you were never able to participate in communion again, would you miss it? Why or why not?

In Other Words

"The Lord's Supper is like a family *re*-union with Christ. It is a . . . meal at which we experience belonging to God and each other in a visible, concrete way and respond with thanksgiving."

—Don Postema, *Space for God*

Live It Out

Tell someone dear to you that you love him or her. Then think of a way to *show* that love—a hug or a kiss or a backrub, an invitation to dinner, or something else.

Session 4
Response
Discussion Guide

One Sunday evening after a college worship service, a young woman student came to me weeping tears of joy. We had heard a wonderful sermon on Isaiah 55 ("Come, all you who are thirsty . . . delight yourselves in the richest of fare") about God's steadfast love: over the top, more than we need, super-abundant, offered free of charge to those who can't earn it and don't deserve it. Then we had celebrated communion. The table had been piled to overflowing with loaves and loaves of bread, a picture of prodigality, and the pastor had encouraged everyone as they ate not to be stingy but to "break off a big chunk of grace."

When I asked this young woman why she was weeping, she explained she had never really understood how God's grace worked. "But you've been baptized, and you've gone to church all your life. Hadn't you ever heard this good news before?" I asked her.

"Well, yes," she replied. "I've heard it. But that's not the same. I had never seen it. I'd never *touched* it."

This week we examined the parts of a worship service that are usually considered responses to the proclamation of God's Word. We explored intercessory prayer as part of our priestly role and considered the offering as our way of signifying that we offer our whole selves to God. We talked about how worship is expansive and sacramental. In different ways, these two adjectives speak to the fullness of our response to God: we worship with the whole church everywhere and in all times, and we worship with our whole selves, body and soul.

Today we follow up on our exploration of the Lord's Supper by studying the three dimensions of time that come together as we feast: past, present, and future.

For Starters
(10 minutes)

Discuss these questions, or something else sparked by the daily readings:

Share a particularly memorable experience (or series of experiences) of the Lord's Supper. Do you remember a time when the sacrament was especially meaningful for you? Have you ever seen or participated in an unusual celebration? Feel free to share frustrating or boring experiences too.

Focus
(5 minutes)

Read the introduction to this session, and then have someone read the following focus statement aloud:

This sacrament is a feast of remembrance, communion, and hope. We come in *remembrance* that Jesus took our sin upon himself and died on the cross in order to save us from our sin. We come to have *communion* with this resurrected Christ—in the elements of the bread and wine and in our fellowship with all Christians who are members of the one Body. We come in *hope,* believing that this bread and cup are a promise and foretaste of the feast of love of which we shall all partake when his kingdom has fully come, when we shall see him, and each other, face to face.

> **Word Alert**
>
> Both Passover and the Lord's Supper are "commemorative" feasts. We do them *in remembrance*. This is more than simply calling to mind a past event. It means to make present an object or event or person from the past. So when Christians "do this in remembrance," we meet and celebrate our glorious, living Savior!

Word Search

(20 minutes)

The following Scripture passages address the three aspects of the Lord's Supper (remembrance, communion, hope). **Read aloud the following Scripture passages and briefly discuss the questions under each (or formulate better ones of your own).**

- Luke 22:14-23
  Jesus says he has been eager to eat the Passover with his disciples. They are observing a Jewish custom they all know very well. Jesus places himself in the place of the lamb sacrificed at Passover and declares a "new covenant."

  This supper was already a time of remembering for the disciples. What were they remembering? What do we remember when we follow Jesus' instructions to "do this"?

  Do you believe that Jesus still "eagerly desires" to share this meal with us?

- 1 Corinthians 11:17-34
  Paul gives the "words of institution" in verses 23-26, explaining why the church observes the supper. Surrounding these verses are Paul's admonition to the church at Corinth, which is struggling with what it means to be a community. Paul's warning is not to eat or drink without "recognizing the body of the Lord."

  In the context of verses 18-22 and 33-34, what does it mean to fail to "recognize the body of the Lord"?

  How might you "recognize the body" in your congregation's celebration of the sacrament?

- Isaiah 25:6-8

  This is one of many places in the Bible where the culmination of God's purpose for creation is described as a great and rich feast; a celebration of death's final defeat and the end of all sorrow.

  Think of some other places in Scripture where a rich feast is a picture of God's final restoration of all things.

  How can our Lord's Supper celebrations express the joy and hope of these sorts of feasts?

Bring It Home
(15 minutes, or as time allows)

Choose *one* of the following options:

Option 1
Invite a member of the group to **think of an especially meaningful experience of the Lord's Supper** in your church or elsewhere. Why was it so meaningful?

Option 2
Does it matter how we celebrate this sacrament? **Discuss what difference it makes** if we stand or sit or kneel, come forward or stay in place or make a circle, break loaves or pass little squares of bread. Are some ways "better" than others?

Option 3
"Dress" a table. **Invite everyone to place three objects and/or drawings on a table to represent what communion means to them.** One object or drawing can represent remembrance, one communion, and one hope.

Pray It Through

(10 minutes)

Let your prayer follow the contours of remembrance, communion, and hope.

- Give thanks for God's saving work throughout history, and in particular for what Christ did in giving us the new covenant.

- Pray for communion in your congregation: each member with Christ and with each other.

- Pray that the kingdom may come and give thanks for the promises that we will share in the great banquet feast of the New Creation.

Live It Out

(10 minutes)

If your group did option 2 above, take home your objects/drawings and keep them in a visible place this week.

If you did option 1, have someone write down the main points of the discussion and pass them along to your pastor or worship committee.

Web Alert

Be sure to check out the participants' section for this session on our website, www.GrowDisciples.org, for interesting links and suggestions for readings and activities that will deepen your understanding of worship.

Sending Forth

Live Wet 1

"As a prisoner for the Lord, then, I urge you to live a life worthy of the calling you have received. Be completely humble and gentle; be patient, bearing with one another in love. Make every effort to keep the unity of the Spirit through the bond of peace. There is one body and one Spirit, just as you were called to one hope when you were called; one Lord, one faith, one baptism; one God and Father of all, who is over all and through all and in all."

—Ephesians 4:1-6

My mother is a wonderful preacher, and over the years my father has become a wonderful listener to sermons. He's especially good at making sure Mom remembers the practical side of things. If Mom gets caught up in theology and imagery and story and forgets to bring it down to earth in her sermon, Dad will complain afterwards: "Give me something to do, Marty!" he says. "I want to leave church with an assignment!"

Practical preaching is a good thing, of course. But even beyond that, the worship service should conclude by sending us out into the world with some marching orders. The "charge," as this part of the service is traditionally called, is an essential part of the final phase of worship: the sending.

We gather for worship, we hear God's Word, we respond in prayer and offering and meal, and then God sends us back into the world. Sometimes this transition point isn't given much attention; the congregation sings a song and the pastor says something like "See you next week!" That's a shame, because the ending of a service is just as important as its beginning. It's where we remember the connections between the three circles of worship, where we begin to test whether our worship was "good." Are we transformed into greater Christlikeness? Are we living into the sacramental glory we have

Word Alert

Remember the *three circles of worship* we started with in the very first daily reading of session 1? We talked about worship as all of life, worship as the hour on Sunday morning when we gather for a worship service with our congregation, and worship as an intimate sense of God's presence.

glimpsed? Does the Word work itself out in our walk? Our worship, in other words, must bear fruit in our witness.

Sometimes the charge is a simple biblical sentence: "Go in peace to love and serve the Lord," or "What does the Lord require of you? To act justly and to love mercy and to walk humbly with your God" (Micah 6:8). Sometimes the charge addresses the particular themes of that week's service and sermon (these are the kind Dad likes best). Sometimes we hear a charge and make promises in response, or we ask God to help us: "Lord, as we go now to our homes and work, by the power of your Holy Spirit, open our ears to . . . our eyes to . . . our hands to . . . and our lips to . . ."

In the charge, the congregation is reminded to live differently—to live wet, that is, as those who have been baptized. In the words of the apostle Paul, "Live a life worthy of the calling you have received." Live like someone who's forgiven, like someone who has

"Belongs to Jesus" stamped on her forehead. Live like someone who knows what it means to die and to rise with Christ, putting off sin and putting on new life.

Connecting the charge with baptism reminds us that even as we receive the "to do" list for the week, we live faithfully and fruit-fully—not so that God will love us but because God *already* loves us. We are transformed by the power of the Holy Spirit, not by our own ability to try really, really hard.

Gratitude for God's work in us also explains why sometimes the charge ends with doxology, or praise to God: "Now to him who is able to do immeasurably more than all we ask or imagine, according to his power that is at work within us, to him be glory in the church and in Christ Jesus throughout all generations, for ever and ever" (Eph. 3:20-21). That means we don't face a week of muddling along in a world apart from God's presence. Instead, we are empowered in worship to bear witness everywhere we go that God "is over all and through all and in all."

Think It Over

1. Think of other occasions in which the final words of the event serve as marching orders. A meeting? A coach's pre-game huddle? A family shopping trip (Billy, you get the eggs; Marie, you get the pancake mix . . .)?

2. What would be missing if this charge were neglected?

In Other Words

"Our sense of identity plays a key role in our behavior, our psychological health, and our spiritual well-being. Baptism, as a sacrament of identity, says to us every day, you are a son or daughter of God. You are loved. In your identification with Christ, the true and perfect human, God is well pleased with you."

—Leonard J. Vander Zee, *Christ, Baptism, and the Lord's Supper*

Live It Out

Read the following charge, a combination of parts of Paul's letters:

> Go out into the world in peace:
> have courage;
> hold on to what is good;
> return no one evil for evil;
> help the suffering;
> honor all;
> love and serve the Lord,
> rejoicing in the power of the Holy Spirit.

Get a Post-it note and pick one or two of these phrases for your "to do" list today. Label the list "Live Wet." Post it where you will see it (at your computer workstation, on the dashboard, the kitchen cupboard, and so on).

Did It Take? (Worship Is Formative) 2

"And we all, who with unveiled face contemplate the Lord's glory, are being transformed into his image with ever-increasing glory, which comes from the Lord, who is the Spirit."

—2 Corinthians 3:18

Earlier that morning, my children had taken inventory of the breakfast goodies that would be waiting for them when we returned from church. As we climbed into the car after worship, they began to tease each other about who would get the cinnamon roll with the most icing on it. Miriam thought because she was the oldest it was rightfully hers. Jacob argued that his work in the yard meant he deserved it. Philip, the youngest, didn't really have a good reason, but when his siblings pointed that out, he had the perfect eight-year-old's rejoinder: *So?* Soon the slightly playful teasing turned into not-at-all playful quarrelling, each of the children demanding their own way—a contemporary version of the disciples arguing about who was the greatest in the kingdom of heaven.

When kids (or parents, for that matter) bicker on the way home from church, does that mean that worship didn't "take"? We've all probably wondered about this problem. Isn't worship supposed to make us better people?

Transformation, though, does not take instant effect. It takes time—a lifetime, in fact. Anyone who has ever tried to stick to a diet and exercise program has a better picture of this. Real and lasting transformation takes effort and persistence and lots of patience.

We often think of worship as a place where we express our love for God, as an outpouring of the heart flowing from our very depths. This is true, and it's a helpful corrective to worship that seems formal, rational, and in-sincere. But we are not the only ones "expressing" in worship. God speaks too. And like Moses atop Mount Sinai, like Zaccheus on his perch in the sycamore tree, like the disciples on the road to Emmaus, we will surely be changed by this encounter with the living God.

> **Word Alert**
>
> When we worship, we do more than *express* ourselves; we encounter the living God. This cannot help but leave us changed—energized, admonished, comforted, empowered to live out our worship in the world.

The nature of the change for each of us will depend upon what is most needed in our lives. Sometimes people speak of worship as "getting my spiritual batteries charged." But that metaphor assumes that worship puts us back where we were before: it's a recharge. Encounters with God have a more complex character—sometimes blessing or disturbing or comforting or admonishing. Most often the transformation worship brings about in us will have the character of Christ and the mystery of death and resurrection about it: our old selves drown in the waters of baptism and our redeemed selves slowly emerge. Or emerge again. And again and again.

But worship is not all about personal transformation. The changes effected by our encounter with God are not changes for their own sake, but *for the sake of the world.* Our souls are shaped for the lives we lead, the service we render, the worship we present to God during the rest of the week.

Think It Over

1. How might you be different if you had never gone to church?

2. What might your parallel universe, non-churchgoing, untransformed self be like?

In Other Words

"Our baptism in the strong name of the Trinity is our confidence of our God, our identity, and our belonging. Our baptism is our calling . . . to embrace and participate in the triune God's own mission to the world."

—Philip W. Butin, *The Trinity*

Live It Out

The next time you shower or bathe, dress, and check yourself in front of the mirror, think of this as a picture of transformation. Pray that God will continue to transform your spirit too.

Play the Song! 3

*"May the grace of the Lord Jesus Christ,
and the love of God, and the fellowship of
the Holy Spirit be with you all."*
—2 Corinthians 13:14

We always sang "My Friends, May You Grow in Grace" at the end of the evening worship service. But this week my college student worship leaders decided we would do something different. After a beautiful, meaningful, concluding song sequence, I raised my hands and said to the congregation, "Go in peace!" Everyone just stood still. Many stared in befuddlement or turned to their neighbors, asking what was going on. "Go in peace!" I suggested a little more urgently. Some people begin crossing their arms. And their expressions. We played the last verse of our carefully chosen new song again, thinking surely they would get the hint this time. Everyone sang out, we finished, and once again I pleaded: "Go! In peace!" Nothing. Then a low murmur began to build until someone cupped his hands to his mouth and yelled loudly: "Play the song!"

He meant the usual one, the one we always sang. And we realized that we had to give the people what they wanted—a blessing. No doubt the students wanted to sing that song partly because of tradition and ritual and comfort. But no doubt they also understood that we need a blessing if we are going to face the world again after worship. We need to receive God's blessing, and we need to pass that blessing on to others.

In session 1, we considered worship as a dialogue, a covenant encounter between God and God's people. Because of this, God has the first word in worship, inviting us to be formed into the body. Not surprisingly, God also has the last word in worship—a word of grace. We have our marching orders from the charge, and God follows up our assignment with blessing—which we can ride like a wave back into the world.

This final word of grace is called the benediction. When we think of how blessing works in the Bible, we realize that such words are not empty or formulaic. Instead they make something happen. Isaac, tricked by his wife and son, gave a blessing to Jacob he'd meant for Esau. And he couldn't take it back. I'll say it again: Blessing words *do* something. God's words of blessing at the close of worship convey God's promises of grace, God's power to overcome sin, God's presence no matter what may happen.

> ─(Word Alert)─
> *Benediction,* **the common term for the final blessing in worship, means "good word" or "to speak well of."**

Most often, a pastor speaks words from Scripture as a blessing. Consider, for example, the blessing from Paul to the Corinthians at the beginning of this reading or the words Moses speaks to the people at the end of his life: "The LORD bless you and keep you; the LORD make his face to shine on you and be gracious to you; the Lord turn his face toward you and give you peace" (Num. 6:24-25). The pastor may also choose to compose a scripturally-informed blessing that gives the congregation a word of blessing particular to that day and to them. A sermon on welcoming the stranger, for example, may lead to a blessing along these lines: "May you always know the peace of your heart's true home in the presence of God."

These words of blessing might be spoken from one person to another. But when spoken or sung in worship, they are God's words to us. In our speaking of them, God blesses us, and we, in turn, become conduits for God's blessing.

In some church traditions, only an ordained pastor may speak for God, pronouncing the closing benediction while raising both hands, palms out, as if it were flying from heaven through them to the congregation. I've often thought about how we as the congregation might physically receive this blessing. Should we raise our hands and catch it? Or pass it to one another with a holy kiss, as Paul recommends in Thessalonians? Most people just bow their heads, a stance that shows appropriate humility and receptiveness.

But perhaps we could think of better (more sacramental) ways to show with our bodies that we receive God's blessing and pass it along to each other and to the world. Maybe we could have one hand out to catch it and lay the other on the shoulder of the person next to us.

At our college worship service, we clasped hands and sang to each other God's words of blessing: "My friends, may you grow in grace, and in the knowledge of our Lord and Savior." Then we raised our hands together, still clasped, and sang praise to God for all God's blessings: "To God be the glory, now and forever, amen." Maybe praise is the best response of all.

Think It Over

1. What's the difference between wishing someone well and blessing them?

2. When do you hunger for the blessing of another person? Of God?

In Other Words

"May God's goodness be yours,
and well and seven times well.
May you spend your lives:
may you be an isle in the sea,
may you be a hill on the shore,
may you be a star in the darkness,
may you be a staff to the weak;
may the love Christ Jesus gave
fill every heart for you;
may the love Christ Jesus gave
fill you for every one."

—Iona Abbey Worship Book

Live It Out

When someone asks you how you are doing today, follow an African-American Christian custom, and say, "I'm blessed." Find an opportunity to bless someone else today, perhaps a child. If you and the other person are comfortable doing so, lay a hand on the person's head or shoulder as you bless them.

"'I have much more to say to you, more than you can now bear. But when he, the Spirit of truth, comes, he will guide you into all the truth.'"
—John 16:12-13

My sisters, as I've mentioned before, are both actors. They both studied with the Second City improvisational theater troupe in Chicago. Want to know the secret of how actors keep their bearings when they're making up skits on the spot? It's this: they're not making it up. Not entirely, anyway. They're following a script.

It's not a script that tells them what words to say—for that they rely on their own quick thinking and sharp wit (and lots of practice). But before any performance, the players work out the overall structure for each skit. For example, a three-minute improv sketch might have three primary movements or "beats." The first will feature some sort of misunderstanding between two of the characters. ("Did you just call me a *cheesemaker?!?*"). In the second beat, tension rises up when something physically explosive happens—maybe one character jumps into another's arms or thwacks another over the head with a pretend sockeye salmon. Finally, the skit ends with a warm reconciliation. The actors know these three beats, and within that form they have the freedom to improvise, to do their own thing. ·

Worship has a script too. We've been studying its broad "beats": Gathering, Word, Response, Sending. We've also been looking at a few "sub-beats" and the typical ways they are expressed. Some congregations follow a pattern for worship that is

very tightly scripted. Other congregations follow the script more loosely, allowing the worship leaders and worshipers the freedom to be expressive, to improvise. Both types of congregations sometimes have an inappropriate sense of superiority about their way of doing things.

Of course, both groups are half right. The notion that the Holy Spirit can only work through spontaneity ignores the fact that God turned chaos into cosmos—ordered Creation—through the Spirit hovering over the waters. The Spirit inspired the highly structured Psalms and the prayer Jesus gave his disciples to pray. But Scripture also speaks of the Spirit inspiring—spontaneous expressions of praise and providing wisdom and courage when they are most needed.

I know from my own experience and from the testimony of many others that the Spirit comes to worshipers and worship leaders in both form and freedom, in both structure and spontaneity. We needn't choose one or the other. In fact, doing so is a bit dangerous.

The same holds true for the all-of-life worship we offer outside the sanctuary. It too is Spirit-led in both form and in freedom. We are given the impulse to approach God not by our own power but by the Spirit. It is the Holy Spirit who guides and gifts us, comforts and blesses and disturbs us, reveals Christ to us, and prays on our behalf when we are unable. The question, then, is not *whether* our worship will be led by the Holy Spirit, but *by what means* the Spirit will lead us.

The "beats" of our Sunday worship guide our daily lives and offer patterns within which we can improvise our days—patterns of praise and petition, of confession and reconciliation, of speaking and listening to God, of giving thanks and offering ourselves, of blessing. As we do these things again and again, the Holy Spirit grows in us the fruit of the Spirit: love, joy, peace, patience, kindness, gentleness, goodness, and self-control. And as these come to rule our hearts—as we become more sanctified—the less we need scripts at all. Our very hearts beat with the heartbeat of the God the Holy Spirit.

Think It Over

1. When do you feel most inspired, most led by the Spirit?

2. How do you tell whether the inspiration you feel at a particular moment is from the Holy Spirit or from some other source?

In Other Words

"May the mind of Christ, my Savior, live in me from day to day, by his love and power controlling all I do or say.

May the word of God dwell richly in my heart from hour to hour, so that all may see I triumph only through his power.

May we run the race before us, strong and brave to face the foe, looking only unto Jesus as we onward go."

—Kate B. Wilkinson, 1925

Live It Out

How would you characterize your congregation's worship? Is it tightly scripted or more spontaneous? Next time you worship, pay attention to the "beats" of worship and think about how you can incorporate those patterns into your daily life. Be as concrete and specific as you can.

The Liturgy After the Liturgy 5

> *"And what does the Lord require of you?*
> *To act justly and to love mercy and to*
> *walk humbly with your God."*
> —Micah 6:8

I have a friend from Arkansas who plays guitar and sings folk songs—which wouldn't surprise you if you saw him. You might not expect, though, that he is also a pastor and worship expert. He likes to greet people—in airports and restaurants and any public place—with a big hug and a Southern drawl, saying "Peace be with you, brother!" or "Peace be with you, sister!" If he knows the folks he's greeting are Christians, he expands a little: "The peace of Christ be with you!"

This is one of the many ways my friend connects Sunday worship with daily life. We greet people in worship with Christ's peace not because we *like* them, or because we are angling to ask something of them; we greet them with Christ's peace because we have been given Christ's peace, undeserved. It reminds us that we are all connected; we're not to see each other as means to pursuing some other end. So if we greet fellow Christians by passing Christ's peace in worship, why not remind ourselves of those truths in the airport or at the grocery store?

Of course, there are many other ways in which we can let our experiences in worship transform our lives outside worship. Once the worship liturgy is over, the liturgy *after* the liturgy begins.

When we go through the actions of worship with attentiveness and an open heart, the practices work on us and prepare us for life outside the sanctuary. Consider these examples:

- The sequence of confession, forgiveness, and reconciliation trains us for the many daily instances in which we must say we are sorry and seek forgiveness.

- Listening and responding to God's Word in worship makes us more attentive to how God speaks, and teaches us practices for our own devotions.

- Praying for ourselves and others, for the whole world, gives us practice for the habit of daily prayers.

- Giving our offering develops in us an attitude of service and self-giving.

- In the sacraments, we see ordinary things as transparent to God, and the death-and-resurrection pattern of baptism and the Lord's Supper is imprinted on us.

- In receiving God's blessing we learn to be a blessing.

We frequently read in the prophetic books of the Bible about God's judgment on the people of Israel when they brought all the right sacrifices to the temple but never got to the heart of worship: a life of justice, mercy, and companionship with God. Jesus had the same complaint about some of the religious leaders in his day.

All our careful worship practices—our well-rehearsed choir anthems, our inventive children's sermons, our roof-raising praise songs—none of it means anything if it doesn't pour out of the hour or two on Sunday and into the rest of our lives.

In our worship we learn what the kingdom of God looks like. We learn to recognize its coming here and now, we learn to long for its fulfillment, and we learn how to be citizens. We practice the song of the kingdom in our worship, and it stirs our hearts to love, our hands to justice, our minds to truth, our lives to peace. We are drawn toward heaven, toward our final destiny with God and God's people. We are not there yet, but we tune our hearts at the door. Sunday worship is the liturgy before our all-of-life liturgy, before our eternal life liturgy and our final blessed future.

Think It Over

Choose one of the bullet points above and consider how practicing that part of worship has changed something specific in your character or life.

In Other Words

"By saying that corporate worship is the 'most real' part of our week, I mean that in it we are in touch in an intense and powerful way with the patterns of the Kingdom of God. The actions we perform and the way our minds, language and emotions are formed in our performance of the liturgy are at the heart of our lives as Christians. In the liturgy, in our worship, we are not simply being presented with information, much less simply being entertained; rather we are being made into Christians—our actions and lives are being linked to the life of the world, our hearts to the heart of God, our minds to the Truth."

—David Stubbs, *A More Profound Alleluia*

Live It Out

We've spoken of daily life as the "liturgy after the liturgy." The one helps you do the other more profoundly. In a similar way, you could think of all these studies about worship as the "liturgy *before* the liturgy before the liturgy." Take time today to review all the "Live It Out" segments from the past weeks and find one that really helped you to worship better on Sunday. Resolve to do that same exercise regularly.

Sending Forth
Discussion Guide

One of the things our family would love to change about our house is the entry. Our front door leads into a teeny tiny foyer, and the front closet is directly across this space from the door so that the two doors bang into each other. When people come over, we have to do a little dance to get them in the house, open the closet, get their coats off and hung up, and get all the doors closed again.

It's even more awkward when it's time to say goodbye. Everyone knows that the sign of a good party is when guests linger by the door, not really wanting to leave. This is hard to do at our house because we all have to stand very close together, like forks in a cup. When the time finally comes for hugs and goodbyes and coats, we're back to that awkward dance. It would be nice if we had more space to do the ending right.

As with parties, so with worship.

This week we considered the final sequence of a worship service, acknowledging that good endings are just as important as good beginnings. Doing the ending right in worship means giving it enough space—in time and in thought. Having called and gathered us into a body and spoken to us in the Word, God receives our grateful response and then sends us out into the world with a charge and a blessing. These parting moments are important: they help us begin to make connections between worship and all of life.

We also considered this week how the practices of worship become places where the Spirit can transform us, preparing us for the liturgy *after* the liturgy in which we become signs of the coming kingdom to the world and fit our hearts for heaven.

Today, to conclude our study, we explore one of many important passages of sending in the Bible: Jesus' "Great Commission" to his disciples.

For Starters
(10 minutes)

Allow members of the group to **share their thoughts about how their practice of worship has transformed them.** Perhaps you can describe your imagined parallel-universe self from day 2 of this week. As a follow-up, invite people to share how they would like God to continue this transforming work, either of themselves as individuals or of your congregation. Or invite group members to share insights from this week's daily readings.

Let's Focus
(5 minutes)

Read the introduction to this session; then have someone read the following focus statement aloud:

After their life-changing encounter with Jesus during his ministry, the disciples are given a mission of multiplication. They are instructed to translate what they have learned from being with Jesus into a world-transforming way of life; they are to teach others and to invite them by baptism into this new life. Jesus gives them the blessing of his promised presence.

Word Search
(20 minutes)

Read aloud the following Scripture passage and briefly discuss the questions below (or formulate better ones of your own).

- Matthew 28:18-20
  Jesus gives the disciples their marching orders, but the authority remains his. The three main verbs in the instructions are *make disciples, baptize,* and *teach.* The Trinity is the identifying name to which the baptized belong. Jesus concludes with a promise of his presence.

  We often think of this passage as a call to missions, which it is. But evangelism is more than simply speaking the message of the gospel. How does one make a disciple? How did Jesus make disciples?

  The phrase from the text—"all nations"—includes our own nation, congregation, family, and self. In what ways do you personally make disciples in this complete sense?

  In what ways do we sometimes forget about Jesus' authority and sustaining presence, acting as if the church is ours to protect and grow and control?

Bring It Home
(15 minutes, or as time allows)

Choose one of the following options.

Option 1
What does it take to be a disciple of Jesus? **Make a list of the five most important character traits and the five most important practices.** How does worship at your church help people gain those traits and practice those habits?

Option 2
Discuss the following questions as you have time:

- In what ways do you find that weekly worship equips you for worship and service the rest of the week? Maybe it doesn't equip you very well. Why not?

- Discuss how your church's service usually ends. Is it really a "sending?" How might it be crafted to better send the congregation into the world as disciples and to make disciples?

- Does the benediction bless you?

Option 3
Ephesians 6 describes the "armor of God." Instead, pack up the backpack of God. **If you could give worshipers at your church a backpack full of "equipment" for their work in the world, what would you put in it?** Don't be too literal; feel free to use symbolic objects or write words down.

Pray It Through
(10 minutes)

Let this sending litany be your prayer. If you wish, have one person speak the "Go" sentences, and have the rest respond with "Alleluia." You might leave a time of silence between each section, allowing people to enter that silence with their spoken prayers.

Go to the world! Go into all the earth;
go preach the cross where Christ renews life's worth,
baptizing as the sign of our rebirth. **Alleluia!**

Go to the world! Go into every place;
go live the word of God's redeeming grace;
go seek God's presence in each time and space. **Alleluia!**

Go to the world! Go struggle, bless, and pray;
the nights of tears give way to joyful day.
As servant Church you follow Christ's own way. **Alleluia!**

Go to the world! Go as the ones I send,
for I am with you till the age shall end,
when all the host of glory cry "Amen!" **Alleluia!**

Live It Out

(10 minutes)

Look for a time this week when you can find a way to bring your worship to an unlikely place. For instance, you might say a silent blessing for someone you see at the bus stop.

> ## Web Alert
>
> **Be sure to check out the participants' section for this session on our website, www.GrowDisciples.org, for interesting links and suggestions for readings and activities that will deepen your understanding of worship.**